Teachers Are Sculptors

Books and Booklets By J.P. Vaswani

In English:
The Seven Commandments of the Bhagavad Gita
Kill Fear Before Fear Kills You
Swallow Irritation Before Irritation Swallows You
Its All A Matter of Attitude
You Can Make A Difference
101 Stories For You and Me
108 Pearls of Practical Wisdom
108 Simple Prayers of a Simple Man
108 Thoughts On Success
114 Thoughts on Love
A Child of God
A Day with Dadaji
A Mystic of Modern India
Begin the Day with God
Beloved Dadaji
Conversations with Dadaji
Dada Answers
Daily Appointment With God
Daily Inspiration
Doors of Heaven
Education: What India Needs
Feast of Love
Five Fragrant Flowers
From Darkness Into Light
From Hell to Heaven
Glimpses
Glimpses Into Great Lives
God In Quest of Man
Hinduism
How to Have Real Fun Out of Life and other Talks
How to Make Your Life A Love Story
How to Overcome Temptations
How to Overcome Tensions
I Have Need of You
I Luv U, God!
Invest in the Child
Joy Peace Pills
Laugh Your Way to Health
Life After Death
Life is A Love Story
Love and Laugh!
Nestle Now
Notes from the Master's Lute
Pictures and Parables
Positive Power of Thanksgiving
Prayers of a Pilgrim
Prophets and Patriots
Sadhu Vaswani: His Life and Teachings
Little Lamps
Secrets of Health and Happiness
Shanti Speaks
Snacks for the Soul
More Snacks for the Soul
Stories for Meditation
Stories for You and Me
Teach Me to Pray
Tear-Drops (poems)
Temple Flowers
Ten Commandments of A Successful Marriage
The Holy Man of Hyderabad
The Kingdom of Krishna
A Little Book of Life
A Little Book of Wisdom
The Little Book of Prayer
The Little Book of Service
The Little Book of Success
The Little Book of Yoga
The Little Book of Freedom From Stress
The Magic of Forgiveness
The Simple Way
The Story of a Simple Man
The Way of *Abhyasa* (How to Meditate)
Ticket to Heaven
Twinkle, Twinkle Tiny Star
What You Would Like to Know About *Karma*
Whispers
Why Do Good People Suffer?
You Are Not Alone!
You Can Be a Smile Millionaire
Destination Happiness
Ladder of *Abhyasa*
Peace or Perish – There is no Other Choice
Good Parenting
The Perfect Relationship: Guru and Disciple

In Hindi:
Ishwar Tujhe Pranaam
Prarthna Ki Shakti
Alwar Santon Ki Mahaan Gaathaayein
Atmik Jalpaan
Atmik Poshan
Bhale Logon Ke Saath Bura Kyon?
Chitra Darshan
Dainik Prerna
Krodh Ko Jalayen, Swayam Ko Nahi
Mahan Purush Jeevan Darshan
Santon Ki Lila
Mrityun Hai Dwaar Phir Kya

Published by
Sterling Publishers Private Limited

Teachers Are Sculptors

J. P. Vaswani

Sterling Paperbacks

STERLING PAPERBACKS
An imprint of
Sterling Publishers (P) Ltd.
A-59, Okhla Industrial Area, Phase-II, New Delhi-110020
Tel: 26387070, 26386209; Fax: 91-11-26383788
E-mail: sterlingpublishers@airtelbroadband.in
ghai@nde.vsnl.net.in
www.sterlingpublishers.com

Teachers Are Sculptors
© 2008, J. P. Vaswani
ISBN 978 81 207 3732 7

All rights are reserved. No part of this publication may be reproduced, stored in a retrieval system or transmitted, in any form or by any means, mechanical, photocopying, recording or otherwise, without prior written permission of the original publisher.

Printed and Published by Sterling Publishers Pvt. Ltd., New Delhi-110 020.

Contents

Author's Preface 9	The Teacher Is A Sculptor 57
The Lamp Lighters Of Humanity ... 13	The Teacher Is An Artist 64
Soldiers Of The Ideal 18	Wanted: Champions 70
Seven Essential Virtues 23	Teaching And Learning – The Current Scenario 75
Two Centres Of Character Building 27	Hold Your Head High 80
Teaching Is Not Just Lecturing 32	Believe And Achieve 85
The Pursuit Of Excellence 36	Work Not For Wages! 90
New Education 42	What Our Students Must Be Taught 96
The Teacher Is A Friend 47	The Evolution Of The Spirit 103
The Teacher Is A Builder 52	The Art Of True Living 108

A Great Sculptor

Michaelangelo, hailed as the greatest sculptor of the Renaissance, believed that all great works of art originated from inner inspiration. While lesser artists fussed over the quality and size of the marble made available to them, Michaelangelo saw potential for great sculpture in every piece of marble. It is said, that his magnificent statue of David was sculpted from an old, abandoned piece of marble, which had been discarded as unfit for sculpture by a minor artist, forty years earlier.

Michelangelo believed that every piece of stone had a sculpture within it; and that the sculptor's job was merely to free the form that was already in the stone.

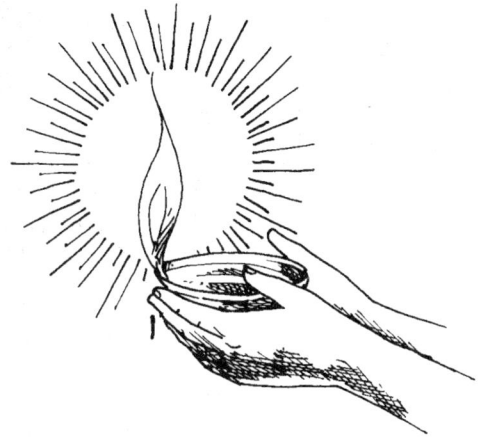

Gather knowledge for service: gather knowledge and be ready for that true life, which is one of offering – the life of *yagna*.

Sadhu Vaswani

Author's Preface

Dear friends and fellow-students...

I hope you won't take it amiss that I am writing a book specially for *teachers*, and choose to address you as fellow-students!

My beloved Master, Sadhu Vaswani, once said to me: "Always remain a student." I have kept this teaching close to my heart; and the day on which I have not learnt something new, I regard as a lost day indeed!

Like all of you, I have passed through the hands of many teachers, from the kindergarten class to postgraduation. In the lower classes we had just *one* teacher – our class teacher – who taught us all the subjects. As we grow up, subject experts take over, and we have Science Teachers, Maths Teachers, History Teachers and English Teachers. In college, there are Professors, Lecturers, Tutors and Demonstrators...

Everyone has to have several teachers – but we remember only a few, while others are forgotten. Even their names are forgotten. Have you ever wondered why this is so?

If you have studied under a teacher whom you still remember with love, affection and reverence, you are truly blessed!

And if you are a teacher who has had such an impact on a student that he/she remembers you for years after his/her education is completed, then you are truly blessed!

I recall a moving incident in the life of the great American author, James Michener. He was once invited to be a guest at a banquet hosted by President Dwight Eisenhower at the White House – a great privilege for any American.

James Michener declined the invitation with regret. In his letter to the

President, he explained, "A wonderful teacher who taught me how to write is being honoured on the same day, at the same time...you will not miss me at your banquet, Mr. President, but she might, at hers."

"Ike" (as Eisenhower was popularly known) was so moved, that he wrote back:

> Dear Mr. Michener,
> In his lifetime a man lives under 15 or 16 presidents, but a truly fine teacher comes in his lifetime far too rarely...

Mark these words: in his lifetime, a man may live under several presidents and prime ministers: but he rarely comes across a truly fine teacher!

They tell me that the age of the 'teacher-less classroom' is here! There is talk of e-learning in a virtual classroom. An interactive computer, they say, can give you all that the teacher can – and without a teacher's strict discipline and eccentricities.

With the greatest respect to technological advances, may I offer my humble opinion that this can never be 'education' in the true sense! Instruction may be offered through the virtual classroom; information may be made available through the computer. But teaching is much more than this: teaching in its truest sense is communicating – a process in which the personality of the teacher interacts with the personality of the students. You can go to a library and read hundreds of books; you can collect data from the Internet; you can listen to recorded lessons on CDs; but can any of these compensate for the living, moving presence of a good teacher?

Let me share with you the words of Swami Vivekananda:

> He alone teaches, who has something to give, for teaching is not talking, teaching is not imparting doctrines, it is communicating... All teaching implies giving and taking, the teacher gives and the taught receives, but the one must have something to give, and the other must be open to receive.

An average teacher instructs; a good teacher guides; a great teacher inspires.

I am sure each one of you can be a great teacher – a source of inspiration and enlightenment to your students!

Let me end this prefatory note – and begin this book, dedicated to you, the ideal teacher, with the *Shanti-path* which occurs in the *Upanishads*:

Sahanavavatu Sahanou bhunaktu

Sahaveeryam karavavahai tejaswina vaditamastu

Mavidvisha vahai –

Om Shanti Shanti Shanti!

May He protect us both (the teacher and the taught) together (by revealing the light of Knowledge). May He nourish us both (by offering to us the fruits of knowledge). May we both acquire energy (through this education): May we both become illumined (through this education); may we not quarrel with each other. Om Peace Peace Peace!

— **J. P. Vaswani**

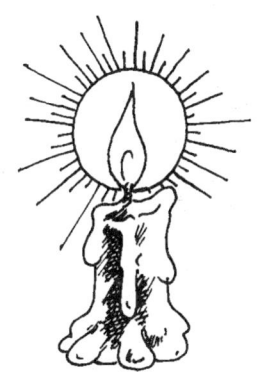

A teacher is a radiant man. He transmits light: he is a man of character.

Sadhu Vaswani

Sensitive Jewels

A tourist was looking at the display in a famous Delhi jewellery store. Exquisite emeralds, rubies and diamonds dazzled the eye. But his attention was drawn to a dull stone, completely lacking in lustre.

"That's certainly not as beautiful as the rest," he exclaimed.

"Just a moment," said the jeweller, taking the stone from the tray and closing his palms around it. Moments later, he opened his palm and the stone glowed with beauty. "This is an opal," the jeweller explained. "It's what we call a sensitive jewel. It needs only to be held with a human hand to bring out its radiance and lustrous beauty."

The Lamp Lighters Of Humanity

Let us begin with a little introspection: who, according to you, is a good teacher?

May be, you would like to complete the following statement by writing down the words or points which you would use to describe a good teacher.

A good teacher is one who...

1.

2.

3.

4.

5.

Now, can I ask you something? When you were writing down the qualities that 'good' teachers possess, were you thinking of your own teachers, whom you admired and respected? Or, were you thinking of abstract, ideal qualities?

The CIEFL, Hyderabad, carried out a survey among fresh graduates, B.Ed. students and others on this subject. Given below are some of the responses they elicited:

A good teacher is one who –

1. Has a thorough grasp/ understanding of his/her subject
2. Takes pride in his/her profession
3. Is a good classroom manager
4. Is a role model for students
5. Understands and respects students and learns from them
6. Has a patient, understanding approach and encourages students
7. Prepares students well to face the exams
8. Prepares students for real life — over and above the exams

9. Relates learning to the real life-needs of the students
10. Is hard working, sincere and dedicated
11. Is humane, sensitive and sympathetic
12. Makes learning fun
13. Is innovative and experiments with new strategies
14. Pays more attention to weak students
15. Evaluates his/her performance regularly

Obviously, each person has his/her own values, beliefs and ideas on what makes a good teacher.

These include

* Personality traits
* Attitudes
* Values
* Knowledge
* Professional experience/skills

Of course, these 'criteria' listed by the respondents are subjective and impressionistic. But the question remains: how can personal traits and attitudes be translated into effective classroom techniques?

And then, there is the question: can good teaching be learnt or taught? Does this involve only a set of skills/techniques? Can everyone become a teacher?

I am no expert on education; I am not here to teach you skills or techniques. But I do believe that teachers evolve, grow with experience, and learn constantly in their ministrations. And this book is not just about *good* teachers, but *ideal* teachers.

I believe each one of you can and must become an ideal teacher!

Reflect... and Act

Congratulations!

...For being one from the fraternity of teachers!

...For belonging to the community of our unsung heroes and heroines!

Your profession is a challenging one! You not only face the difficulty of teaching the subject to many unwilling learners, but also undertake to tune in with a hundred different, diverse personalities all at once!

As you took up the vocation of being a teacher, you were probably faced with tremendous challenges:

o teaching the subject

o maintaining discipline

- preparing teaching aids
- coping with overwork
- attending staff meetings
- participating in the cocurricular activities of your institution
- dealing with tough and demanding principals and relentless parents
- very little credit or appreciation
- burn-outs on the personal front
- working into the nights at home
- constant hassles with corrections, mark sheets, report cards

...the list can go on. For all the colossal commissions you have undertaken, you can stand tall and pride yourself for choosing this profession.

Why?

You know this deep within...this is the most rewarding and enriching of all human experiences, which is to impart knowledge to another! Teaching moulds your personality, strengthens your convictions, teaches you patience, love and acceptance.

In A Lighter Vein

When asked for her occupation, a woman charged with a traffic violation said she was a schoolteacher. The Judge rose from the bench. "Madam, I have waited years for a schoolteacher to appear before this court." He smiled. "Now, sit down at that table and write 500 times, "I will not pass through a red signal."

Education should be related to life, and not be an academic study.

We must aim at an integral education in which humanism is blended with the spiritual ideal. Education must teach students to stand up as soldiers of the ideal.

Sadhu Vaswani

I Am Not Educated!

Dr. Albert Schweitzer, the distinguished humanitarian and Nobel Laureate, had just started his relief work in the backwoods of Africa. Toiling all by himself, he would fell trees and carry the logs of timber on his strong shoulders. Log by log, he singlehandedly endeavoured to raise the walls of his hospital building.

One day, struggling with a particularly heavy load, he spotted a black man nearby.

He hailed him, "Brother, can you give me a helping hand?"

"Hey Mister," came the haughty reply, "don't you know, I am educated?"

Dr. Schweitzer smiled and said, "I am happy *I* am not educated!"

Soldiers Of The Ideal

I am not going to try and define education for you – you probably have your own favourite definition, and you may even have your own strong views on what education is all about. But I do wish to share with you the views of my Master, Sadhu Vaswani.

As some of you may know, Sadhu Vaswani had a brilliant academic career, standing first in his college and winning prestigious awards and scholarships. He began his teaching career in the Metropolitan College, Calcutta, from where he moved to the D.J.Sind College, Karachi. Soon, he became Principal of the Dyal Singh College, Lahore. Later, he took over as Principal of the Victoria College, Cooch Behar, and finally became the Principal of Mahendra College, Patiala.

Much later, in 1933, he founded the MIRA Movement in Education, based on his well thought out ideology, aimed at cultivation of character through the ideals of simplicity, service, purity and prayer. Education should be for life, not livelihood, he felt; and to this end, he conceptualised a system of education which would integrate the head, hand and heart.

May I tell you, I often think that modern education has sharpened the brain, the mind of our youth – but in the process of making youngsters smarter, more efficient, more intelligent, more competitive, it has somehow hardened their hearts!

Let me share with you an incident narrated by a leading educationist and thinker. He was travelling from Mumbai to Delhi, and his co-passenger was a smart, handsome engineer, who was travelling to Delhi on his first job-interview with a multinational. The two of them struck an easy companionship and had an interesting conversation on several issues.

"What are your plans?" the older man asked his young friend. "A smart young lad like you can achieve anything you set your mind on!"

"Well, Sir, I am quite ambitious," the young man admitted. "I am very keen to get into a multinational and work abroad for sometime."

"What next?" asked the senior man.

"Hmm...in about five years I would like to have a house of my own in Mumbai ... you know, it can be done if one is earning in U.S. dollars."

"Of course, of course. What then?"

The young man said, a little self-consciously, "Get married, by the age of thirty. In my community, the best girls with the best background and the best dowry are available for NRIs – so I can take my pick!"

"How interesting! What next?"

"O Sir, you know what's next. Start a family, have kids...and I'm determined to send them to the best schools and the best Universities in *the world!* Of course, it is going to cost a lot of money, but I'm determined I'll give them the best education – it is my investment for their future!"

"What then?"

"What then? Retire on a fat pension and enjoy life – what else?"

"What then?"

The young man was startled. "What then?" he repeated blankly. "Nothing!"

Is that all there is to life – make money, get married, beget children, *buy* their education – and beyond that, nothing?

Tateh kim? Tateh kim? asked Adi Shankara, centuries ago. What then? Is making money the be-all and end-all of education?

In the year 1944, Sadhu Vaswani was invited by Pandit Madan Mohan Malaviya to visit Benaras Hindu University. At a gathering of teachers and students whom he addressed, a question was put to him: "What are the marks of a truly educated man?"

In answer, Sadhu Vaswani said, "The truly educated man is even he, who expresses the life force within him, and who has in some measure, won real freedom."

Ya Vidya Sa Vimuktaye – so our ancient scriptures tell us. *That* is knowledge, which liberates you; if you are enslaved by materialism at the end of your education, can you call yourself liberated or educated?

I invite you to ponder on the words of Mahatma Gandhi:

> Getting by heart the thoughts of others in a foreign language and stuffing your brain with them, and acquiring some University degrees, you consider yourself educated? Is this education? Open your eyes and see what a piteous cry for food is rising in the land of Bharata, proverbial for its food. Will your education fulfill this want? The education that does not help the common mass of the people to equip themselves for the struggle for life, which does not bring out strength of character, a spirit of philanthropy, and the courage of a lion – is it worth the name?

Let us ask ourselves – the education we are offering our students today – is it worth the name? Are we merely stuffing their minds with facts – and neglecting their hearts? Are we drawing out the life-force that is within them? Are we giving them true freedom?

Reflect... and Act

Do Your Duty – And A little More!

When you carry out your duties in the spirit of an offering to God, you grow in the awareness that His Will is working through you, and this makes even difficult tasks easy.

Here are a few suggestions that will help you grow in the spirit of *karma yoga*:

- Cultivate the quality of selflessness – it only requires a little love, a little compassion, and a little sympathy. Selfless work also promotes inner joy and peace
- Conquer the lower emotions like anger, egoism, jealousy and envy
- Cultivate self-control over your thoughts, words and deeds
- Learn to be amiable and adaptable. Accommodate yourself to others – especially colleagues and students
- Do not develop rigidity about what you can do and what you do not want to do. As a teacher, you cannot say, "I shall lecture, but I cannot supervise examinations; I cannot evaluate answer papers"
- Learn to fit into any kind of situation or environment in your class, in your institution
- Develop a balanced approach to life and people
- Always be polite and courteous in your dealings with others
- Accept criticism in the right spirit
- Avoid aggression and imposing your will on others
- Appreciate others' concerns; look at problems from their point of view
- Do not find fault with others. Learn to see the good in all. Appreciate your colleagues and students – and learn from them
- Avoid arguments, gossip and idle talk
- Do not be half-hearted in your efforts. Put in your best, give your 100% to whatever you do

And why, you might ask, am I expected to be so rigorously 'noble'? Why can't I just do my job and be done with it? Why should I aspire to *karma yoga* ?

The answer is very simple: you are not just another employee, just another professional; yours is not just another career. Yours is a vocation – an avocation. You are a teacher – and people look up to you for ideals and standards.

In A Lighter Vein

"The teacher said that I must learn to write more legibly," the child told his mother. "But if I do, she'll find out that I can't spell."

To *educate* is to develop the character and individuality of a pupil – the mind, will and soul-power of the student.

Sadhu Vaswani

I Eat It With A Fork

An American expert, during the course of his expeditions, encountered a group of cannibals. They were about to sit down to a feast of human flesh. Imagine his surprise on being told that the cannibal chief had actually studied in an American University!

In sheer astonishment, he said to the cannibal chief, "You have studied in an American College and still eat human flesh?"

The cannibal chief quietly answered, "Yes. The only difference is that I now eat it with a knife and fork!"

Seven Essential Virtues

Michele Borba is a distinguished educationist, best-selling writer and motivational speaker. In her book *Building Moral Intelligence*, she outlines what she calls "Seven essential virtues" which we need to inculcate in our youngsters, so that they may face the challenges and pressures of life successfully. She calls them "the core virtues…that will nurture a life long sense of decency" in our students. These virtues are:

1. *Empathy* – which will allow them to understand others' feelings. It will make them sensitive, caring and compassionate.

2. *Conscience* – which, with its unfailing inner voice, will help them discriminate between right and wrong choices. It will guard them from temptation and make them judge their own actions fairly.

3. *Self-control* – which will help them to discipline themselves and prevent them from excessive indulgence in any form. It will also teach them the quality of sharing – so that they learn to serve those less fortunate than themselves.

4. *Respect* – which will enable them to learn from others and give due deference to points of view other than their own narrow perspective. This is the basic foundation for human rights.

5. *Kindness* – which will bring out the best in them, nurturing qualities like compassion, service and sacrifice. It will also cure them of the deadly sin of selfishness.

6. *Tolerance* – which will enable them to appreciate and respect differences in people, faiths, beliefs and opinions. The society of the future is undoubtedly a multicultural society – and it cannot do without tolerance.

7. *Fairness* – which will help deal with others impartially and justly. It will teach them to respect rules, and treat all people equally.

To this I would add the twin qualities of humility and reverence which, together, constitute the hall-mark of every truly educated person.

Can we say that it is *not* the teacher's business to inculcate these qualities in the students? Can teachers wash their hands of moral values altogether?

Reflect... and Act

Incorporate Life Skills In Your Teaching

Most students look up to their teachers, more than anyone else. A teacher's influence lasts forever. Therefore many crucial life skills which go untaught even by the best of parents can be taught by teachers. This includes not merely traditional areas like moral science, but also issues related to family, relationships, health and diet, etc.

Even if you are a Science or a Mathematics teacher, your opinions on all these issues will shape the personality of your students.

Do you refer to any of these issues in class?

- The importance of family and how to treat everyone with love and respect
- The importance of courtesy and kindly speech to everyone who crosses our path
- The need for a healthy diet and courage to give up junk food
- The value of our great Indian culture and heritage and the misleading influence of western culture
- Taking care of our body, treating it with respect and the effects of its abuse
- Spirituality and what God and the Universe mean to your students. The importance of God in our lives. Also inculcating a bond/relationship with Him
- Respecting all castes, religions and different socio-economic groups
- Knowing oneself and what one wants from life
- Setting goals for the future
- Developing a healthy sense of self esteem without being arrogant/egoistic
- Service of the poor and the under-privileged

In A Lighter Vein

When one teacher told his class to write the longest sentence they could compose, a bright kid wrote : "Imprisonment for Life."

New India will be built not in the *Lok Sabha* or the *Rajya Sabha* but in the home and the school!

Sadhu Vaswani

TWO CENTRES OF CHARACTER BUILDING

Unity

I dreamed I stood in a studio
And watched two sculptors there,
The clay they used was a young child's mind
And they fashioned it with care.
One was a teacher:
The tools she used were books and music and art;
One was a parent
With a guiding hand and gentle loving heart.
And when at last their work was done,
They were proud of what they had wrought,
For the things they had worked into the child.

— Ray A. Lingenfelter

Two Centres Of Character Building

Everyone would agree with the idea that parents are a child's first teachers: however, they teach the children in the course of their life, through everyday experiences. They teach the children responsibility; they give them values; they help them develop self-respect; they help children widen their horizons...in fact, teaching flows naturally from good parenting.

However, this is not to undermine or devalue the teacher's role, which is very distinct. And I for one, would not agree with the view that value education stops with the school, while 'higher' education should be more 'professional' or 'objective': names and labels should not deter teachers from doing their best.

What are the aims of education? Alas, for many parents and many students, this aim is severely limited: education is meant to secure a well-paid job.

A friend from Chennai expressed the regret that the best students were no longer opting for the pure sciences in Madras University: their first choice was invariably medicine or IT or biotechnology, or at least commerce – all of which were perceived as being assurances of a safe and secure future.

This friend carried out an informal interview with parents: and he found that parents were even more swayed by social perceptions than the students! The attitude seemed to be like this: "If my daughter/son studies physics or mathematics, everybody will think she/he was not clever enough to get into medicine/engineering."

There seems to be some confusion here. In their obsession with 'professional' education, the parents themselves fail to see that postgraduation/research in chemistry or physics can also lead to a high-paying job – for qualified specialists are becoming a rarity in these subjects.

This also points to a more fundamental misconception about 'profession' and 'education'. The purpose of a profession is to provide a means of earning one's living. As for education – I think most of us would agree that it is to make one cultured and civilised.

Can a teacher at the school or college level, afford to ignore this basic aim of education? Can he or she say, "My job is to teach Biology/Chemistry/Sociology/English/French. I cannot take on the role of a Godparent or Moral Guardian for my students?"

If a teacher has this attitude, I think he/she is short-changing students – not giving them what they need, what they must get.

Your teaching will remain incomplete, if you do not reinforce the knowledge you impart with your own personal wisdom.

Your teaching will remain incomplete, if you do not contribute in some way to the personal development of your students.

Learning should not be fettered by the single aim of *earning*. As the ancient Sanskrit verse tells us:

> O Goddess of Learning, Your treasure is unusual; the more it is spent, the more it increases; if one stores it, it becomes extinct!

Where knowledge is hoarded, learning departs. The vast wealth of knowledge is only accumulated by those who are continuously inspired to learn more, and to share all they have learnt with others.

A teacher is not a paid employee who does a stipulated job within stipulated hours. A teacher's objective must not be merely to help his students pass examinations.

I believe every teacher can be – and must be – an agent of personal development, individual growth and social transformation. Each student in your class has, in a sense, entrusted his future in your hands. This is a great privilege, an honour – and a tremendous challenge and responsibility.

Do you not owe it to yourself and your students to rise to this challenge?

Reflect... and Act

Do Little Things Well!

It's the simple stuff that makes up a great teacher: here's what a few children had to say on why they love their teacher:

I Love My Teacher because...

- o I love my teacher because she writes big and clear on the blackboard
- o I love my teacher because she understands when I am confused

- I love my teacher because she notices when I say "please, ma'am"
- I love my teacher because she admits she made a mistake
- I love my teacher because she smiles when she knows I have worked hard
- I love my teacher because she doesn't mind going over the explanations again and again

In A Lighter Vein

The teacher of the school geography class was lecturing on map reading.

After explaining about latitude, longitude, degrees and minutes the teacher asked:

"Suppose I asked you to meet me for lunch at 23 degrees, 4 minutes north latitude and 45 degrees, 15 minutes east longitude...?"

After a confused silence, little Jagdish volunteered - "I guess you'd be eating alone!"

There is a hidden *shakti*, a life force in every pupil. And it cannot be drawn out by repression or fear. Environment is an important factor in the development of the child.

Sadhu Vaswani

TEACHING IS NOT JUST LECTURING

My Teacher Can Talk...!

Two boys were bragging about the abilities of their teachers.

"I'll bet my teacher can talk one hour on any subject," said one.

"Huh!" replied the other fellow proudly. "My teacher can talk for one hour without a subject."

Teaching Is Not Just Lecturing

Educational researchers tell us that many teachers rely on the age-old 'lecture' method for teaching their subjects. They add that many teachers actually take great pleasure in 'lecturing' to large classes.

Once upon a time, 'lecturing' was regarded as the best method of teaching – especially when text books and reading materials were not freely available or accessible to the students. Perhaps a lecture is still the best method to teach content based subjects: this is why our universities rely largely on the lecture-system, even in postgraduate classes.

Unfortunately, the lecture method is often based on some problematic assumptions:

1) The teacher knows exactly what has to be taught.

2) The 'lecture' is the best way to prepare students for examinations.

3) In this system, one of the important functions of the teacher is maintenance-of-discipline or 'classroom management'.

4) This entails that the teacher restricts her position to the front of the class, instead of moving about freely.

5) The learner in this system must necessarily be a Listener – with a capital L.

Granted, many teachers may be extraordinary subject-experts, offering valuable inputs to the students in their area of specialisation. Their knowledge of the subject has been gathered from many sources over many years, and it is their task to disseminate this knowledge among their students in the most efficient and systematic manner.

As one teacher put it to me with great feeling: "It is all very well to argue that the teacher's job is *not* just to help the students pass examinations. But if a majority of our students *don't* pass their examinations, do you know who will be held responsible by the institution and the authorities?"

True! Very True! But it is also true that while 'subject experts' may be remembered with awe, it is teachers who have offered guidance, support and inspiration who make a lasting contribution to the students' well-being and development.

Let us recall the unforgettable words of William Arthur Ward:

> The mediocre teacher tells
> The good teacher explains
> The superior teacher demonstrates
> The great teacher inspires!

Reflect... and Act

Remember - You Are Their Role Model

It was a wise man who said:

"Teaching by example is not just one way of teaching, it is the only way."

Never forget that as a teacher you are their greatest role model. Your words, actions, qualities are being absorbed in a subtle way into their subconscious minds. So be alert and aware of yourself, even your thoughts!

- o Take care of your thoughts, they become actions
- o Take care of your actions, they become habits
- o Take care of your habits, they become your character
- o Take care of your character, it becomes your destiny.

We can add, for teachers:

- o Take care of your thoughts, they indirectly affect the lives of all those around you!

In A Lighter Vein

A fourth-grade teacher was giving her pupils a lesson in logic. "Here is the situation," she said. "A man is standing up in a boat in the middle of a river, fishing. He loses his balance, falls in and begins splashing and yelling for help. His wife hears the commotion, knows he cannot swim and runs down to the bank. Why do you think she ran to the bank?"

A girl raised her hand and asked, "To draw out all his savings?"

The noble Eastern tradition has taught us that education is a thing of the spirit, that money is not the measure of a man – and that schools and colleges are meant to be centres of light.

Sadhu Vaswani

A Considerable Achievement

Members of five hundred learned societies from all over the world, got together to organise the 250th Birth Anniversary of Benjamin Franklin. The commemorative conference had to be divided into ten different sessions to do justice to various aspects of Franklin's genius:

1) Science, invention and engineering;

2) Statesmanship;

3) Education and the study of nature;

4) Finance, insurance, commerce and industry;

5) Mass communication;

6) Printing, advertising and the graphic arts;

7) Religion, fraternal organisations and the humanities;

8) Medicine and public health;

9) Agriculture;

10) Music and recreation.

Franklin was truly a great man, a well-rounded personality who took an interest in everything that was happening around him! Yet we have reduced his achievements to the dimension of the lightening-and-kite-string experiment, because it is easy for us to grasp!

The Pursuit Of Excellence

There was a time in India, when teachers were venerated as Gods: *He who taught me to read and write is the equivalent of God*, is one of the famous sayings by the Tamil Saint-poet Avvaiyar. Students were considered to be metaphorically blind, until the teacher opened their eyes to the world of knowledge and wisdom.

Despite the change in attitudes and values, teaching continues to be regarded even today, as a vocation, rather than as another 'profession'. True, like many other countries, we passed through a period of student unrest and indiscipline, when many teachers were made to feel that theirs was no longer a 'noble profession'; that society and institutions and perhaps even the people did not give them the respect that was their due. On the one hand, they did not really belong to the highly-paid category; on the other, they were made to feel that they were just doing a paid job – like clerks or managers or supervisors. Many good teachers suffered from a tremendous loss of morale. Unfortunately, many wrong, inappropriate people who regarded teaching as 'just another job' also got into the profession, leading to compounded confusion and misunderstanding.

The commercialisation of education in our country has brought with it, its own attendant problems. The plus point here, is that the growing number of private institutions are offering educational opportunities to many more students; ensuring much sought-after careers and jobs to several well-qualified teachers. My friends tell me, that under the new order of WTO, 'education' is now regarded as a 'service' and new global implications will soon emerge for all our academic institutions.

I may add here, that people of my generation, have always regarded education as a 'service' – not a 'service industry' as WTO specifies – but as a great *seva*, a social service offered by the educated, enlightened teachers, who chose the noble task of spreading the light of education. This is why we in India, have always regarded our teachers as light-givers, votaries of Goddess Saraswati, in truth, *gurus* in the academic sense.

"We are certainly not *gurus*, we have no right to regard ourselves in such a light," a teacher protested to her friends, when the students of their college organised a special *Guru Poornima* tribute to all the teachers.

I would disagree with her view! It may be true that *spiritual gurus* are to be distinguished from the academic profession, but in truth, every teacher should hold herself in high self-esteem as a *guru*. If she sees herself and her profession in this light, she will certainly achieve standards of excellence for herself and her students.

In a sense, 'teaching' is all about self-perception. If I regard myself as a drudge, a lowly servitor doling out data, facts and theories to a bunch of youngsters whom I don't like – why then, I am a misfit; one of those unhappy people who is grounded in misery, forced to do an unpleasant job for the sake of a living. If there are such people in the teaching profession – and my eternal optimism tells me that there cannot be *any* – let me say to them, "Choose a job you love, and you will not have to work even for a day in your life!"

I think this is what the best teachers do – they have chosen a job they love – and they do not regard teaching as work!

A distinguished Professor once told me: "A good teacher loves his profession, loves his subject and loves his students. Even if one of these is absent, he cannot be good at his job."

Certain recent trends in our country have been welcomed by all right thinking people: not only has the UGC revised the salaries and scales of teachers in colleges and universities, they have also tried to raise the standard of recruitment by stipulating strict eligibility norms and qualifications.

If Indian education is to retain its ancient status as *Vidya*, we must treat our teachers well and give them the respect and regard they deserve.

And if our teachers wish to be more than mere purveyors of knowledge, if they wish to retain the high stature of *gurus*, their single-minded goal must

THE PURSUIT OF EXCELLENCE

be the pursuit of excellence in all that they do.

Since independence, we have had several Commissions and Reports on the state of education in the country. If I mistake not, the first Education Commission was headed by none other than Sarvepalli Radhakrishnan – the eminent philosopher, statesman and educationist, whose Birth Anniversary (Sept. 5) we now observe as Teacher's Day. From the Radhakrishnan Commission up to the present, our best thinkers and civil servants and teachers have striven to set standards of excellence that is worthy of a nation which worships knowledge and learning in the form of the Goddess Saraswati.

The Acharya Ramamurthi Commission, which submitted its Report in the late 1980's, had a very important point to make. Taking due note of the various suggestions and recommendations made by previous education reform commissions; and also taking into consideration the general sense of dissatisfaction and discontent that was becoming widespread in the education system, Acharya Ramamurthi made a very pertinent suggestion: students, teachers and all stakeholders who felt that improvement was needed, should not wait for the system to change; they should not look to the Government, to the Universities or to the authorities to *bring about* reforms: instead, they should just go ahead and *practise* excellence in teaching and learning! If more and more people did this, excellence would be achieved in the system automatically!

What an inspiring suggestion this is! Why should others set standards for you? You can set your own benchmarks – and if all of you do your best, give of your best to the profession and to the student community, would you not be ushering in a new age of enlightenment in Indian education?

Reflect... and Act

You Can Make A Difference!

Remember that a good teacher can change her students, and in due course, the world!

It is so easy to give in to despair, when you look around see the anarchy, indiscipline, violence and cynicism in all areas. It would seem that we cannot do much to alter the situation – but a good teacher can make a difference! You can make a promise to do your little bit to usher in an era of peace, love, honesty, truth and prosperity for all. This can be achieved if the communities of teachers vow to go that extra mile to make a paradigm shift in value education. If one student can be influenced positively, he in turn reaches out to so many lives!

It is crucial that a teacher must realize once and for all that his/her profession has more potential than the politicians to shape the future of the nation. In order to change the world we have to begin with ourselves. It is men and women of inner conviction who can influence the world around them.

Therefore :

- o Connect with your highest Self
- o Develop a sense of self-esteem
- o Take pride in your vocation
- o Adopt a proactive attitude in your class
- o Spread positive vibrations wherever you go
- o Become an agent of change for yourself and others around you

In A Lighter Vein

Teacher: History is a very interesting subject. It tells you about what had happened in the past.

Student: Please teacher, I don't think I want to study history.

Teacher: Why?

Student: There is no future in it.

The true educator is a teacher of the "Guru" type – an inspirer, not a chastiser of students. He is clothed with the authority not of the rod, but love.

Sadhu Vaswani

The Flower And The Seed

A teacher was giving her primary class a talk on flowers. "Now children," she said, "who can tell me what makes the flower spring from the seed?"

"God does it," answered one little girl. She paused and added, "and the loving care of the gardener!"

New Education

Sometime ago, I met a well-known academician. Not only had she served as the Vice Chancellor of a University, but had also been deputed to the Ministry of Education at the Centre, on a special delegation. At that time, a New Education Policy was being drafted. She discussed the details of the Policy with me and observed that the New Policy was really good, and that it filled her with a lot of hope and optimism for the future.

I said to her, "The policies may indeed be very good – but what is more important to me, are the men and women who are going to implement them."

I have said this several times in the past – and I will say this again and again – the one urgent, the one great need of India today, is teachers of the true type: men and women of light, men and women attuned to great ideals, whose magnetism will work better than text books, and whose influence will outlast examinations – which, alas, end in headaches and heartaches for our students.

Yes, we need teachers of the true type – men and women, who, through precepts and examples will impress on their students that life is larger than livelihood; that the end of education is not gains in silver and gold, power and fame, but service and sacrifice. Such teachers will work for the future of their students; such teachers will mould the character of their students; and their work will not easily pass away.

We look back on the pre-independence era and remark sarcastically that the British education system in India was designed to produce a succession of clerks and lower order civil servants to carry out the *diktats* of their white superiors. Let us ask ourselves honestly; are we not now, producing young men and women whose sole aim is a fat salary? Are we not providing canon-fodder for multinationals whose only objective is to multiply their profits? Are we not channelising our best 'products' into the ever out-flowing tracks of brain-drain?

In its truest and deepest sense, education ('drawing out', in its Latin sense) is meant to tap one's highest potential; it must help the students to know themselves; it must help them to realise their essential nature; it must enable them to fulfill the purpose of their life. Students must feel, at the end of the day, that they have done their best not only for themselves, but for the society, the nation and humanity at large.

Here is what Azim Premji, one of India's well-known entrepreneurs says of our system:

There is no doubt that our students are good in academic skills, and some of them have brought great honour to their institutions. Yet, when it comes to a vast majority of students...we are only creating large masses of followers who look to others to tell them what to do with their lives...

How can we create leaders, instead of followers? The British education system was meant for "the ruled", for "subjects". What we need now, are responsible citizens, potential leaders of society, industry, administration and governance. How can we gear our education system, our teaching-learning practices towards this goal?

Reflect... and Act

Take A Leaf From Your Students' Book!

Have you ever wondered why teachers are always young in spirit?

Science has proved that so long as a person continues to learn and evolve, the cells of the body – especially those vital grey cells of the brain – continue their regeneration process. They stop growing once we stop having a mind that is open to new concepts, adapting to fresh ideas, gathering new insights!

Teaching is just what the doctor ordered if one wants to stay young in heart and spirit, even while we evolve dynamically. This is simply because all teachers are sure to learn so much from the young people who meet and interact with them, year after year!

Just consider some of the qualities your students bring into your class – and into your life!

- o Enthusiasm
- o Exuberance
- o Enterprise
- o Vitality

- o Energy
- o Optimism
- o Fun and laughter
- o Creativity
- o Fresh, new ideas

Undoubtedly, teachers will benefit from these positive, youthful qualities – for they are infectious!

In A Lighter Vein

Summer vacation was over and Little Naresh returned back to school.

Only two days later his teacher phoned his mother to tell her that he was misbehaving.

"Wait a minute," she said. "I had Naresh with me for three months and I never called you once when he misbehaved!"

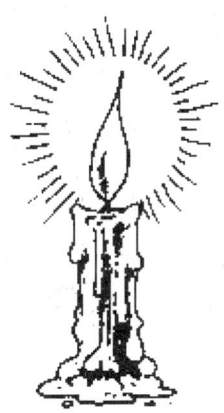

Friendship is the essence of true education. The teacher is a true friend of his pupils – friend and guide.

Sadhu Vaswani

Don't Silence Him!

A professor who had taught for many years, was advising young teachers.

"You will discover," he said, "that in every class there will be a youngster eager to argue. Your first reaction will be to silence him, but I advise you to think carefully before doing so. He probably is the only one listening."

The Teacher Is A Friend

Whenever I am asked – who is an ideal teacher, I hear the words of my beloved Master ringing in my ears. He said to us again and again: The true teacher is a friend!

The true teacher is a friend. He is a friend of his fellow teachers; he is a friend of his pupils; he is a friend of all creation; he is a friend of men, women, children, birds and animals; he is a friend of all who suffer and are in pain.

Yes my friends, this is the one great mark of a true teacher: he is, above all, a friend. It is in an atmosphere of friendship that a teacher can draw out the best that lies within the mind and heart of the pupil.

As we all know, education is derived from the Latin roots, *e-duco,* which means, "I draw out". Education is essentially a *drawing out* process – it is not *pumping* in dry facts and figures into the heads of the students – it draws out that which is already in the students. And this drawing out process is possible only in an atmosphere of friendship.

There is a proverb in Tamil which says: "When your child reaches the level of your shoulders in height, you must begin to treat him/her as your friend." What is true of parents is also true of teachers; those of you in higher education who are teaching young adults must treat your students as your friends.

Let me make it clear that I do not suggest that you 'hang out' with your students or allow them, the kind of needless 'familiarity' which involves back-slapping, first-name terms and exchanging personal confidences! That is *not* what I mean by friendship.

In order to maintain your dignity and stature as a teacher, you have to stop short of such easy familiarity. The kind of friendship I advocate, is more like a benign elder, a protective guardian, a caring mentor – like the all-encompassing, 'friend, philosopher and guide' in that immortal expression!

David Brenner made it in the tough world of 'show biz' in the U.S. He became the Host-Presenter on a Network Show and built a good fan following. When he became a celebrity, he recalled with gratitude his Physics Professor, Dr. Jacobs. As a young man, Brenner had been classified as a 'disruptive' student, who often disturbed and upset classes with his 'funny' tricks and jokes. Dr. Jacobs made a deal with his boisterous student: at the beginning of each class, he would give Brenner five minutes to crack his jokes, to jest around, to do anything he wanted – but just for five minutes! At the end of the five minutes, Brenner would have to sit down, behave himself and follow the rest of the class quietly.

Brenner would always remember the Physics Professor announcing in class: "Ladies and gentlemen, Physics 101 is proud to present the comedy styling and antics of David Brenner!"

Dr. Jacobs was able to channelise the youngster's excess energy, while keeping him in control. Little wonder that Brenner would always remember him with love and gratitude!

You may not all have comedians in your class; but I'm sure you have aspiring singers, artists, sportspersons, painters and dancers! Help them to channelise their energy; appreciate their talents; help them to discover their own potential and still be a useful, productive member of the class.

Dr. Bhatnagar, the distinguished physician, was regarded as a duffer, a poor performer, a below-average student during his college days. The teachers ignored him – and he made himself 'invisible' by becoming a permanent fixture in a dark corner of the last row in class.

One day, a new Professor of Philosophy came to his class. Walking up and down the class to familiarise himself with his students, he came upon the huddled figure, all alone in the corner of the last row. He had been talking to his students about bringing out their best, about achieving their best potential. Continuing the same theme, he said to the huddling student, "There's something great inside you. Unfold it! Do your best to achieve it!"

Dr. Bhatnagar recalled with gratitude that unforgettable day – and the unforgettable Professor, who said those magic words to him. He began to think, for the first time, that there was something in him, after all!

The Professor proved to be right – and Dr. Bhatnagar was inspired to make his teacher's words come true.

The Professor of Philosophy was none other than *Sadhu Vaswani*.

Reflect... and Act

Love Makes The World Go Around!

Therefore, Kahlil Gibran said:.

> *You give but little when you give of your possessions. It is when you give of yourself that you truly give.*

How often it is that many years into our adult life we forget the subject matter of what was taught in school but the memory of a gentle word, a kind gesture, an inspirational talk, a patient explanation from our teachers lingers on? They were the qualities that made a lasting impression on our minds!

It is reassuring to know that no matter how many negative forces are at work in our lives, it sometimes takes no more than one person, one act of love or acceptance or encouragement, to make a difference in our lives!

Historic personalities are only images; fictitious characters only live in the imagination; but a teacher is real! Her influence touches the life of the students!

Here are some of the ideals a teacher can inculcate in the students:

- Truth
- Courage
- Patience
- Hard work
- Kindness
- Dedication
- Commitment

These ideals can be inculcated in the youth of today only through real, tangible people who are none other than the teachers.

In A Lighter Vein

Physics Teacher: "Isaac Newton was sitting under a tree when an apple fell on his head and he discovered gravity. Isn't that wonderful?"

Student: "Yes sir, if he had been sitting in class looking at books like us, he wouldn't have discovered anything."

Put the child right and the world will come out right!

J.P. Vaswani

THE TEACHER IS A BUILDER

Put The Child Right!

A wealthy businessman returned home after a busy day in his office. His nine year old son rushed to the father's side joyfully. He climbed on to his father's knees and begged his father to play with him.

As for the father, he was anxious to catch up with all the day's business news in his favourite newspaper. "Now you must go to your room and play with your toys, because daddy has to read the paper," he said to the boy. However, the son was not willing to leave his father's company. "You come to my room and play with me daddy, please" he begged. "I don't want to play on my own. I like to play with you!"

"Alright, alright," said the father. "I'll tell you what, we will play a little game right here. Do you see this world map here on my newspaper? I am going to cut it into small bits and give it to you. You must try and put it together correctly. When you have done it, I will come up with you to your room and we can both play together. Until then, you must let me read my newspaper. Agreed?" "Agreed!" said the boy eagerly. The father quickly cut the world map in several small pieces and put them before the boy on the floor. Then he settled down comfortably with his newspaper and started reading the business pages.

To his utter astonishment, the youngster was back on his knees in just a few minutes, triumphantly holding up the world map stuck together perfectly with cellotape.

"How did you manage that?" asked his father in sheer surprise. "Did you look at an Atlas to get the world right? How did you put the world map together so easily?"

"I don't have an Atlas," said the boy. "But it was very easy for me to put the world together. Behind the world map there was a picture of a child. I just put the child right and the world came out right!"

The Teacher Is A Builder

Until India achieved political independence in 1947, Indians across the country were inspired, indeed, fired, by a common ideal, so powerfully captured for the public imagination in the immortal words of Lokmanya Tilak: *Swaraj is my birthright and I shall have it!*

But after independence – what? It is not as if we suddenly had no more ideals to live for, no more goals to achieve. Once we realised the cherished dream of becoming a sovereign democratic republic, we faced more problems, more issues than ever before. The Indian Constitution had promised several things to the people; above all, it promised the people, that with freedom, we would set out to reshape, rebuild India according to our own needs, ideals and vision. And there were three major problems that confronted the nation: poverty and backwardness; illiteracy; and caste and communal divisions. It was our national responsibility to work to solve them.

In some ways, after sixty years of independence, the situation has not improved as much as we would have wished in 1947. Our responsibilities still weigh heavily on us, and we are still a long way away from achieving our dream of universal education, removal of poverty, and upholding national integration and harmony.

There can be no true freedom without responsibility. We cannot sit back and say that the Government or the administration or the politicians have failed to solve our problems. It is as much our responsibility as theirs, to face these challenges and overcome them.

I am reluctant to make a generalisation – but I believe that generally people are more conscious of their individual freedom and their *rights* as citizens of India. There is another side to freedom and rights; and that side will show us that we have responsibilities and duties towards the society, the community and the nation. In sixty years of independence, we have still not accepted these responsibilities and duties fully.

The task of nation-building, the stupendous work of achieving real development and progress is before us now. And once again, I recall the words of my Master: "New India will not be built in the *Rajya Sabha* and the *Lok Sabha* but in the home and in the school!"

My friends, do not imagine that I'm burdening the teachers with monumental duties and responsibilities, which even the Government cannot handle. My point is this – we still have crucial lessons to learn; our young people need to be educated in the right manner, to face up to their duties and responsibilities – and who better, than our teachers, to do what they are best at?

All the changes we have made in our educational system were meant to make our education nation-oriented and value-oriented. We have not perfected the system yet – but if it is to succeed in the task of nation-building, it is you, the teachers, who can make it possible.

Education plays a vital function in a democratic system of Government. And it is our teachers who shape, mould and train the minds of our youngsters, thus playing a major role in making them responsible citizens of this country. Though much emphasis is laid on primary education and teaching children, we must not forget that the crucial, impressionable years (from 18-21 and above), which they spend in college, are also of utmost importance.

This places a great challenge as well as a tremendous responsibility on our teachers – but I cannot help thinking that it is also a great privilege! To take up this challenge successfully, to build responsible citizens and to build a new India, the teachers too, must have national goals and Indian values: only then they can pass these onto their students!

The teacher is a builder – not of bridges and buildings and townships – but a builder of men, a builder of minds, a builder of life. Let me remind you of the words of Edwin Markham, who asked:

> Why build these cities glorious
> If man unbuilded goes?

It is man who needs to be rebuilt. And who will build good human beings but the teacher? It is the teacher's sacred task to build the lives of the students who come to him/her. In building their students, the teachers are building the future of the nation!

Reflect... and Act

Respect Your Students

The potential possibilities of any child are the most intriguing and stimulating in all creation.

Ray Lyman Wilbur

Never judge or label any student! History has shown us the example of great, personalities who were misjudged and "written off" by their school teachers. Their potential went unnoticed! Who would like to be remembered in the way Einstein's or Bill Gates' teachers were remembered? They were the ones who labeled these students as unworthy, incapable and uneducable – as 'failures'!

There is always scope for improvement and a change for the better. Tagging a child always limits their growth. Not only do the children doubt their own potential, but they are also distrustful of your lack of belief in their capability. This indirectly limits you from making a positive contribution to their improvement. Statements like " This is all he is capable of" , or "She cannot do it" should be banned from every teacher's conversation!

Remember, every child is a product of many factors like

- o Upbringing
- o Environment
- o Genetics
- o Predisposition

Remember, too, none of these factors are in their control. Make allowances for their lapses; understand their weaknesses; forgive them when they slip!

It is good to remember the wise words of Goethe:

"Look at a man the way he is, and he only becomes worse. But look at him as if he were what he could be, and then he becomes what he should be!"

In A Lighter Vein

A little girl came home from school and said to her mother, "Mommy, today in school I was punished for something that I didn't do."

The mother exclaimed, "But that's terrible! I'm going to have a talk with your teacher about this ... by the way, what was it that you didn't do?"

The little girl replied, "My homework."

The schools and colleges, which do not seek to kindle in the hearts of students the light of sacrifice, are no better than dark prison-cells.

Sadhu Vaswani

True Wisdom

"Can you tell us what is true wisdom?" they asked Plato.

"Perfect wisdom has four parts," Plato replied. "The first is wisdom, the principle of doing things aright; the second is justice, the principle of doing things equally in public and private; then there is fortitude, the principle of not flying away from that which you fear, but meeting it; and finally there is temperance, the principle of subduing desires and living moderately. Together these four parts make up true wisdom."

The Teacher Is A Sculptor

A sculptor wields
The chisel and the stricken marble grows
To Beauty...

So runs an old poem. The art of sculpture is indeed fascinating: with his chiseled touch, the sculptor hews a living shape out of old, lifeless stone, shaping, moulding, carving a thing of beauty out of cold marble.

The educationist and philosopher, Bertrand Russell, makes a very interesting observation about 'individuals'. He says that an individual is rather like a billiard ball – which only knows how to collide with other billiard balls! The point he is trying to make is that too much of 'individualism' only sets men on a collision course against each other. A man who believes in his own *individuality* will find it difficult to cooperate with others and work with them for a common goal. Therefore, our spiritual teachers believed that true growth comes from moulding *personality* rather than just individuality.

Sanskrit and Hindi use two modified forms for *individuality* and *personality*: *vyaktitva* stands for individuality, while *vikasita vyaktitva* stands for personality.

When young people from diverse backgrounds come to your class, many of them are yet to develop a sense of individuality. Teachers first need to give them this sense of individual worth and dignity. But if we stop at this stage, our work will not be complete: an individual is likely to remain rigid, self-opinionated and self centred for life – a billiard ball, ready to clash with other billiard balls.

May be this is what is happening in this so-called age of LPG – an age of materialism, sought to be achieved through Liberalisation, Privatisation and Globalisation. We are ready to stress our rights and fight for what we feel is our due. But we lack social responsibility, civic awareness and emotional maturity.

These qualities can only come from the development of personality – and therefore, I emphasise the teacher's role as a sculptor who shapes and moulds the individual into a wholesome personality.

From *vyaktitva* to *vikasita vyaktitva*, the transformation is achieved through the shaping, moulding power of education. As an individual, a young man or woman is apt to imagine that he or she is at the centre of the Universe, and everything and everyone must dance to his or her tune. It is the teacher's duty to humanise such youngsters, to make them realise that life is not just taking, receiving, grasping, gaining and ordering others. *Growth* is not just physical expansion or even intellectual expansion, but spiritual growth, through assimilation of values. *This,* no text book or degree can bring about – but only a true teacher. This is the difference that Sri Ramakrishna Paramahansa pointed out between the 'unripe ego' and 'ripe ego', which he called *kaccha ami* and *pakka ami.*

How will you shape, sculpt, mould the individual into a wholesome, vibrant personality? We speak a lot about Human Resource Development and HR Management today. Can I put it to you – the entire future Human Resource of this country is seated in the classrooms of teachers like you, across the length and breadth of this country! And it is you, the teacher, who is a living role-model before them.

You can shape them for their benefit and the nation's benefit. You can inculcate virtues and graces in them through precept and example. You can enrich their lives by giving them values.

Education should not stop with promoting physical and intellectual growth; these must lead to character development – only then does the cold, lifeless marble, become alive, beautiful and striking! The 'individual' learns to devote his excess strength, knowledge and power, to serve the nation, to serve other people, to serve the world at large; he ceases to be self-centered. He becomes service-centered!

Sri Ramakrishna narrated a parable to illustrate this distinction between *kaccha ami* and *pakka ami.* A father went to the market and brought two ripe, luscious fruits for his two children. On returning home, he gave one fruit to each child. The elder child took the fruit, went straight to his room, closed the door, ate the fruit, wiped his mouth and then came out to play with his friends in the courtyard.

As for the second child, he took one look at the delicious fruit, went straight out to his playmates in the courtyard and shared it with everyone present.

The elder child was very 'clever' in the material sense, in the ways of this world. He was individualistic, self-centered; he was intelligent enough to look after his own interests.

The second had a less selfish, more mature personality. He naturally thought of others and his first impulse was to share, to give. This is the kind

THE TEACHER IS A SCULPTOR

of attitude we must inculcate in our children!

The aim of education, Sadhu Vaswani said, is not gains in silver and gold. It is cultivation of character, compassion and spirituality in the student. He went one step further and said to us: "India does not need leaders and masters, for there are many willing to take up that role; India needs servants and *sipahis* – and it is for this that we must train our students."

I know that it will not make me very popular to say this to you: but the great ancient ideals of this nation are service and sacrifice – *seva* and *tyaga*. It is these ideals that we must kindle in ourselves, and thereby light up the flame in the hearts and minds of our youngsters. Our managers, authorities, administrators and leaders are already well-versed in the art and science of making money, of *using*, even exploiting people for their own benefit. What we need to teach the younger generation is the spirit of selfless service, the spirit of sacrifice. Please don't shrink from the words sacrifice and service; they are not qualities reserved for ascetics and renunciates. They represent the finest virtues that a well-rounded human being can aspire to; they represent significant points in the spiritual growth of a person. They represent the higher levels of man's evolution and the true progress of civilisation and culture.

This is the most important task before teachers today: sculpting, shaping, moulding our youth into socially responsible citizens; making them good human beings imbued with the virtues of sincerity, committment, dedication, service and sacrifice.

A UNESCO Report of Education had the significant title: *Learning To Be*. Please take note – *Learning To Be,* not learning to do or learning to make – this constitutes the essence of true education: the art of living, the science of true life; not just the art of living in peace with yourself, but the art of living with people; serving people; helping people; and contributing one's best to social and national growth. This is the essence of education as expressed by Swami Vivekananda: "Be and Make!"

Reflect... and Act

Every Student Is Unique!

The aim of teaching – indeed, the aim of education – is not to turn out money-making machines, but to cultivate sensitive, sympathetic, service-minded individuals, to whom life will always be larger than livelihood. It is the considered opinion of experts, that conventional approaches to teaching, is not conducive to this end. For one thing, it is known that conformity can often lead to mediocrity.

It is said that mediocrity can recognise nothing higher than itself; but it takes intelligence, sensitivity and talent to recognise genius. Remember, there may be a potential genius, an unrecognised high performer in your class!

Don't let the constant emphasis on academic success, destroy valuable qualities in your students such as:

- Spontaneity
- Originality
- Creativity
- Independent thinking

Let your goal as a teacher transcend the obvious end of helping your students to pass examinations! Aim to create better human beings, integrated personalities, whose God given intelligence may be put to the best possible use.

In A Lighter Vein

A high school had a policy that the parents must call the school if a student was to be absent for the day.

Kiran (name changed to protect the guilty), deciding to skip school and go to the mall with her friends, waited until her parents had left for work and called the school herself.

This is the actual conversation of the telephone call...

Kiran: "Hi, I'm calling to report that Kiran so-and-so is unable to make it to school today because she is ill."

Secretary at high school: "Oh, I'm sorry to hear that. I'll note her absence. Who is this calling?"

Kiran: "This is my mother."

Needless to say, she didn't pull it off!

The urgent need of India's educational institutions is to cultivate the soul.

I believe that true education must be a unifying force.

Sadhu Vaswani

Bringing Out The Best

The toddlers' class was given a very unusual assignment that day. Their class teacher had told them to draw a leaf on their slates.

The kids bent over their desks, eyes narrowed, foreheads wrinkled in concentration, tongues thrust out sideways, through their clenched lips – their entire energy focused on drawing.

At the end of the period, the teacher came round with his cane, inspecting each boy's drawing. One of the boys had drawn half a banana leaf; he insisted that the other half had gotten out of the frame of the slate. Another boy had drawn an elephant because he said he liked elephants.

The teacher stopped at Laxman's desk. He took up the boy's slate and asked, "What's this?"

"It's a *peepul* leaf," said the boy hesitantly.

The teacher studied the drawing for a couple of minutes and then looked at Laxman. Becoming slightly anxious now, the little boy put out his hand, ready to take the caning, which, he was sure was coming his way.

The teacher held up the slate for the whole class to see. "Laxman gets 10 out of 10 for his drawing," he announced. "You are going to be an artist!" he said to the boy, patting him on his back.

The teacher was right. The little boy who had drawn the lifelike and beautiful *peepul* leaf turned out to be India's best loved cartoonist, R.K.Laxman.

The Teacher Is An Artist

Once, a young girl asked her Guru to tell her about the purpose of her existence. "Tell me Master," she beseeched him, "what does God want me to do with my life? What tasks am I expected to perform?"

The holy man thought for a while, and then bade her to go to a nearby garden and observe the flowers there. "Come back and tell me what you find," he said to her, "and I shall give you the answer to your question."

The girl came back in a short while. "I have seen beautiful, fully formed flowers in bloom," she told the Master. "They are wide open, their petals are a lovely colour, and they are so fragrant. But I have also seen buds which are yet to open – they are not so beautiful, colourful or fragrant. They seem to be waiting for something to happen..."

The Guru nodded in understanding. "The purpose of the bud is to bring out all the beauty and colour and fragrance that it has *inside* itself," he explained to her. "Its purpose is to become a perfect flower."

"You too, are capable of such beauty, such perfection," he added. "Your aim must be to evolve into a perfect human being, an ideal person in whom all the beautiful virtues such as compassion, kindness, service and sacrifice will be manifest...you too, must be in full bloom like the perfect flower!"

If the spiritual unfolding of the pupils is the aim of true education, am I not correct in describing the teacher as an artist who must embellish the beauty of their hearts and minds, so that they may bloom forth in full perfection?

Education, as we have seen again and again, is a matter of inner transformation. Imparting information, passing on theories and techniques cannot help our students to face the multiple challenges of life. What they need are illumined minds, enlightened intellects, inspired hearts: these alone can bring peace and joy to them, and enable them to live their lives fully.

Swami Sivananda tells us:

> Education is not a 'filling in' of something from the outside. It is a drawing out from within, of the highest and best qualities inherent in the individual. It is the cultivation and development of these worthy talents and qualities in an intelligent and rational way, so as to help build a balanced personality.

Does this not require a creative artist of the highest order?

We spoke earlier, of Sadhu Vaswani's description of the truly educated man as one "who expresses the life force within himself." Only someone with creativity can express the life force within; only someone with the creative impulse can identify and bring out the life-force in his students. Creativity is the first mark of the true teacher. Not only is he himself creative, he creates the kind of environment in his class which brings out the latent creative faculties of his students.

Everyone of us, every one of the students in your classes, each young boy and girl, occupies a unique place in the great cosmic plan of life – a place which cannot be taken by any other individual. I cannot fill your place in the great cosmic plan, you cannot fill mine. It is the creative principle, the life force within us, that makes us unique.

Today, wherever we turn, we find only imitation! Our youngsters want to imitate Film stars, TV stars or Pop stars. The young generation of politicians aspire to take the place of their fathers, mothers or godfathers. Every young entrepreneur wants to become a Bill Gates or an Ambani.

One day, a student of philosophy came to meet Sadhu Vaswani. "I have been invited to America, to deliver lectures on the *Bhagavad Gita*," he informed the Master. "I have come to seek your blessings, so that I too, may be another Vivekananda."

Sadhu Vaswani blessed him and said to him, "I don't want you to be another Vivekananda, I want you to be yourself."

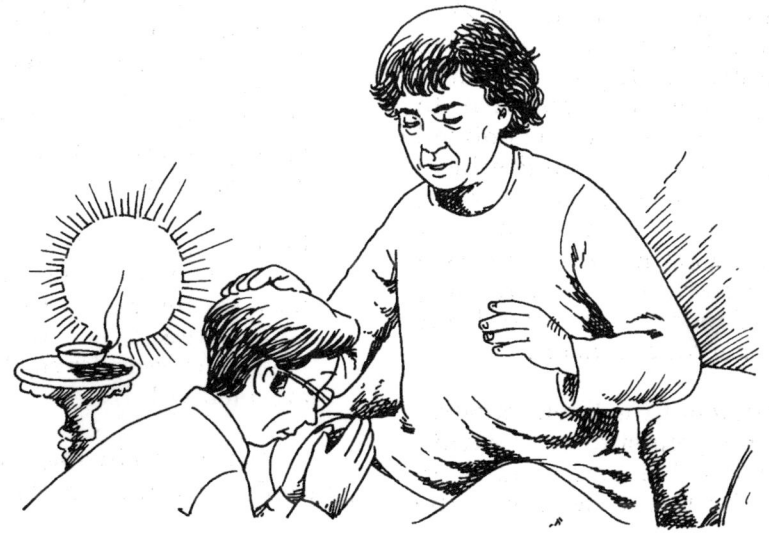

Everyone must aspire to be himself/herself. Everyone must be taught to bring out the creative impulses that are within.

There is a theory that our educational system must meet what is called the "manpower requirements" of the country. True, we need our share of engineers, doctors, nurses, administrators, technicians, biologists, physicists and so on. But we must also spare a thought for society at large: any civilised society needs its share of cultured men and women; liberal thinkers and philosophers who can influence public opinion for the common good; creative artists, writers, musicians and poets and painters, who will add beauty, wisdom and wonder to life; and above all, seekers who will go in quest of deeper truths and also impart them to the rest of us. All these people are being nurtured, taught, trained in your classes. It is the teacher who must spot them, identify them and nurture the creative impulse in them.

Not all students from all classes are going to achieve recognisable greatness; but remember, the vibrancy and sustenance of any civilisation also depends upon the masses of its people; the nameless, faceless middle classes whom we tend to regard as mere consumer statistics. The people must be cultured, sensitive, responsive to social needs – and above all, imbued with at least basic moral and ethical values. Whether a man is a doctor, engineer, pilot, carpenter or businessman; whether a woman is a manager, scientist, researcher, musician or dancer – they should be men and women of character!

When you bring out the latent creative impulses within your students, you are not just moulding their personality. You are shaping the future destiny of the country.

At the level of higher education, you must try to extend their creativity and intelligence in every way possible. Let them find new horizons; let them discover new dimensions of their own personalities! Let them discover their wings!

Here is a distinguished thinker's views on the subject of creativity in education:

> Each second we live is a new and unique moment of the universe, a moment that will never be again...and what are we teaching our children? That two and two make four, and that Paris is the capital of France. When will we teach them what they are? We should say to each of them: Do you know what you are? You are a marvel! You are unique!
>
> In all the years that have passed, there has never been another like you!... you may become a Shakespeare, a Michaelangelo or a Beethoven. You have the capacity for anything. Yes, you are a marvel!

You are not producing standardised, graded articles, nuts, bolts or commodities. You are fashioning human beings; you are helping them grow and evolve to perfection. You are teaching young people to grow strong in creating, reflecting, thinking and achieving! You are fashioning the leaders of the future – and leaders, more than anyone else, need to be creative. Each one of your students has infinite potential, so help him tap the potential, so that the individual may be transformed, and through him, the society and the nation may be transformed!

Reflect... and Act

Raise Your Own Bar!

Don't look to others to set your standards. Create your own benchmark. Evaluate yourself and reach for higher marks, because it is imperative that you assess yourself constantly and make the desired changes in your attitude and approach.. If you feel you need to be more patient, loving, forgiving and honest, then the time to do it is – *now!*

The best way to monitor yourself is to ask for an honest feedback from others. Many schools and colleges now make it a practice to ask students for a teacher-assessment feedback. Your seniors and colleagues could also provide valuable inputs to help you improve in technique and approach.

At the end of each day, write down at least one thing that you feel you have done right—something which gave you a sense of satisfaction, something which you feel, added to your repertoire of being the wonderful teacher you aim to be; some indicator of your growth and development that also works as a feel–good factor.

Here are a few examples from teachers who recorded short messages about their growth;

- o "My patience and tolerance seem to be improving. I kept my cool throughout a particularly tough session."
- o "I am learning to focus on the positive aspects of each student."
- o "My sense of humour stood me in good stead today."
- o "I have succeeded in appreciating every little thing that my students get right."

In A Lighter Vein

The children were lined up in the cafeteria of a Catholic elementary school for lunch. At the head of the table was a large pile of apples. The nun wrote a note, and posted on the apple tray: "Take only ONE. God is watching."

Moving further along the lunch line, at the other end of the table was a large pile of chocolate chip cookies. A child had written a note, "Take all you want. God is watching the apples."

Stand up and fight for life's ideals. Better to fight and fail than not to fight at all.

Sadhu Vaswani

Children Are Seeds

Solon was one of the great thinkers of ancient Greece. He is remembered, even today, as a great lawgiver.

One day, Solon went out among the citizens, holding a rotten apple in his hand.

To the people who gathered around him, he raised the question, "Can anyone tell me what I can do to regenerate this apple – to make it new?"

The people shook their heads in negation. What could one do with a rotten apple? As for making it new – whoever had heard of such a thing? It had to be thrown away – and that was that.

Receiving no answers to his query, Solon cut the apple into four pieces.

Taking the seeds of the apple, he said to them, "The way to make this apple new, to create new apples out of this rotten apple is to sow these seeds. Out of these seeds will bloom forth new apples."

The people marveled at the lawgiver's vision and wisdom. How could they have forgotten that even the rotten apple contained within itself the source of new life – its seeds?

Likewise, when humanity becomes rotten, remember that the seeds of humanity are its children! Invest in them! Take care of them! For they can regenerate humanity!

Wanted: Champions

May I anticipate what some of you are beginning to think at this point? You are probably thinking, "Hmmm...it sounds so good to think of the teacher as a builder, a sculptor, an artist and so on...but Dada seems to have no idea of ground realities! If only he knew what our routine is like! Preparing for undergraduate, postgraduate lectures, conducting seminars and organising student presentations, participating in multiple college activities, carrying out administrative tasks of our own departments – and completing exhaustive syllabuses in each class and preparing students for the examination – where do I have the *time* to build, sculpt, mould and create?"

Let me respond to you – if this is your view. Do not underestimate yourself or your influence! It is said that if the ideal one embraces is worthwhile, then he who embraces it must also be the best and the most worthy among men! You have chosen a noble profession: there can be no two opinions on this, that education is the very foundation of civilisation, human progress and democracy. And all of you, who belong to this noble profession must, of necessity, be noble and wise and great! You uphold, protect and propagate the supreme wealth of *Vidya* – and you are in a class apart. How could I expect anything less than greatness from you?

You belong to a noble profession; you have committed yourself to a valuable mission, which is making a profound contribution to the world. The question should not be, "How much can I achieve?" but rather, "What is it that I cannot achieve, if I set my heart to it?"

You are the children of Goddess Saraswati: and her wealth of knowledge increases as it is shared. You are eternal light-givers, for you are always leading your students from ignorance to knowledge. Yours is the permanent helping hand that is leading the youth on the path of progress and self-improvement. You are a part of the unbroken tradition of knowledge and scholarship that began with the very dawn of civilisation, and will last as long as human civilisation lasts! How can anyone devalue you or your profession? Let me urge you, therefore, to hold your head high, fill your heart with hope and optimism, strive with self-confidence, live and work in a manner true to the ideals of your great vocation – and do everything you can for the young aspirants who have entrusted themselves to your care!

I know we live in an age of cynicism and lack of reverence. But, if anyone can mend matters, it is surely people like you! The world needs men and women of principle and commitment like you. The world needs men and women of wisdom and training, who alone can create true values. Your young wards not only need to be taught the three 'Rs', maths, science, politics, civics, sociology, psychology, computers, commerce, accounts, administration and the languages: they also need to be taught the fine and wonderful art of true living.

The great American philosopher, Ralph Waldo Emerson, stated emphatically: "Justice always wants champions!" We can modify that passionate statement and say, "Education always needs its champions!" The truly capable and gifted scholars are those who nurture and foster others like them. If you are one of those gifted teachers who can train their students to surpass them in achievements and scholarship and in living a life imbued with ideals and high principles – hats off to you! For you have fulfilled your mission, and deserve the highest praise and admiration!

Reflect... and Act

Pay More Attention To Slow Learners

In this age of fast paced learning and cutthroat competition, it is important to know that there are students who need intensive and repetitive teaching.

Every teacher cherishes his/her favourite students – the ones who are

- o always ready with answers
- o always responsive and attentive
- o always at the top of the merit list

True, these students need to be recognised, appreciated and rewarded.

But, remember, the smarter ones will learn even on their own. The slower ones definitely need your patience, encouragement and support! You are the one who can pull them up to match the rest of the class.

Let the slow learners in your class feel that you are on their side, that you are there to bring out the best in them, that if they take one step forward, you will be there to lead them ten steps forward, and help them reach the goal.

When you freely give of your time and effort to encourage slow learners, the class as a whole will feel a tremendous sense of security; for the students will be happy and proud to know that they have a caring, understanding, compassionate teacher, who wishes them well. The students will also imbibe these qualities from you, and become sensitive, kind and responsible. The class as a whole will feel motivated to do better, and their feeling of unity will be strengthened.

In A Lighter Vein

The teacher came up with a good problem. "Suppose," she asked the second-graders, "there were a dozen sheep and six of them jumped over a fence. How many would be left?"

"None," answered little Norman.

"None? Norman, you don't know your arithmetic."

"Teacher, you don't know your sheep. When one goes, they all go!"

Knowledge is increasing: is happiness increasing, too? Schools are multiplying: are happy homes multiplying?

Sadhu Vaswani

Using The Brain

A rich lady bought an expensive electric appliance for her kitchen. The carton contained a manual of instructions to assemble the equipment before use. In her eagerness she spread out all the parts on the kitchen table and tried to assemble the equipment herself. But it all seemed so complicated that she left everything on the table and went away to take a nap.

When she returned after her siesta, she was amazed to see the appliance, fully assembled, on the table, which had now been cleared of all the mess she had left behind. Apparently, her cook / housemaid had put it all together.

"How did you manage to do it?" she asked the maid.

"When you don't know how to read, you're forced to use your brains, Madame," was the reply.

Teaching And Learning – The Current Scenario

Recently, I had the opportunity to meet with a few brothers and sisters from the teaching profession. Some of them had sad accounts to share with me: a few of the more senior teachers suffered from low morale. There was a general lack of optimism and cheer.

My own optimism and positive thinking have never made me blind to the negative aspects of life. I am aware that the teaching profession has changed considerably in the last century or so, and the emphasis on quantity and numbers has brought with it, its own attendant problems.

From the earliest times in India, teachers enjoyed considerable freedom over what they thought and felt and what they imparted to their students. We talk of 'autonomy' as if it were our own invention – but few teachers, few institutions could have enjoyed the kind of autonomy and freedom enjoyed by our *rishis* in their *ashramas*. Just imagine – they did not have to advertise their services and seek emoluments. Kings and nobles, generals and merchants, wealthy men and women and poor householders brought their children to their *ashramas,* and begged for them to be accepted as pupils.

As for the disciples themselves, they lived and worked and ate with the Guru and his family; they served him; they participated in all the chores of the *ashrama;* they fetched fuel and water; they cleaned and washed; and they received the accumulated wisdom and scholarship of the Guru, offered to them in a spirit of reverence and selfless sharing.

Now, teachers have become part of a public service that is offered to the people. They are no longer free to teach what they like or what they wish – but to instill those facts, theories or beliefs that the authorities think suitable. Sadly, in many cases, as Bertrand Russell expressed it regretfully, the teacher has become a civil servant "obliged to carry out the behests" of other men.

But, to my mind, this does not alter the importance of education, or the value of a true teacher. A true teacher has vital functions to fulfill in our society, and you cannot be a great teacher, until you fulfill those functions. To quote Bertrand Russell, once again: "Teachers are more than any other class, the guardians of civilisation."

As C.E.M. Joad put it so well, civilisation is not merely about being rich, eating delicious food and riding in motorcars and flying in planes. Civilisation is a matter of the mind and spirit! It is, above all, an attitude to life, an attitude to the Self, an attitude to progress and values that matter. And our true teachers, our great teachers *cannot* stop with imparting facts and theories: they must impart values. They must foster young men and women, with a civilised attitude!

Reflect... and Act

Learn To Deal With Stress

Find remedies to deal with stress stemming from personal issues, before you enter the classroom. Invariably, it is the suppressed issues that get accumulated and find a vent on defenseless people we come into contact with – in this context, the students. If you, the teacher, feels stress, then the students absorb it subconsciously, and this will influence them – and you – adversely.

Here are some ways to deal with stress:

o Try deep breathing whenever you have time between classes

o When you have a problem, try to talk it over with a friend or an understanding colleague

o If the problem is connected with a troublesome student, then find practical ways to correct the student. Do not use your authority or position to release your displeasure

o When you enter the class, tell yourself, "I am taking God with me into the class."

The most important point to check is this: is your stress related to non acceptance of your job as a teacher or disrespect for your own profession? If that is the case, you should constantly affirm that you love your job and are in an extremely satisfying profession. If you are still unhappy about your work you should consider another profession, simply because your miseries will not be just yours but will become the misery of all your students.

In A Lighter Vein

Teacher: Why are you late, Ramesh?

Ramesh: Because of a sign down the road.

Teacher: What does a sign have to do with your being late?

Ramesh: The sign said, "School Ahead, Go Slow!"

Be strong! Be manly! And let no changes in the fortunes of life affect the interior and the integrity of what you really want.

Sadhu Vaswani

The Best Investment

A rich businessman came to seek his *Guru's* advice on a matter that had been bothering him.

"I have amassed a fortune for my sons," he said to the sage. "My problem is that I do not know what is the best and safe manner to invest it for my children. Gold is not reliable; stocks and shares fluctuate wildly; real estate does not always pay good returns. What shall I do? Where shall I put my money?"

"Give your children the kind of wealth that no one can take away from them," the sage advised him. "Give them the wealth of good education."

It was a wise man who said, "If a man empties a purse into his head, no one can take it from him."

Hold Your Head High

In the early 1990's, a Pay Commission Recommendation was implemented with regard to college teachers' salaries; and, for the first time, their pay scales began to look comparable to the salaries drawn by qualified professionals – though still nowhere near those offered in industry/business.

A college teacher wrote about an appalling experience she had at that time. This lady, an English Lecturer, was the wife of an engineer who worked as a senior technocrat in a private industry. She had accompanied him to a party given by one of his colleagues. Their host was also an engineer, a highly qualified person, occupying a senior position in the same company. In the course of the dinner, the host began to unleash a tirade of abuse against what he called "this needless hike in the salary of teachers." In his opinion, it was unwarranted, undeserved, and a waste of public funds.

"Do you know, a pathetic *English teacher* now gets Rs. 4,000/- as starting salary?" he thundered. Our friend, the English lecturer, nearly dropped her plate in confusion, embarrassment and anger at this outburst. Her host either did not know, or did not care that she herself was one of those "pathetic English teachers". He went on and on, while she and her husband exchanged exasperated glances.

"I tell you, these people don't deserve this kind of pay," he thundered. "For three months in the year, they are on vacation. None of them is ever in college for longer than four or five hours – many of them just sign and leave! They teach for two to three hours a day and they are simply not accountable to anyone."

"Would you rather have colleges without lecturers?" the lady asked him, when she was able to get a word in edgewise. "Or would you keep them permanently underpaid and overworked, the dregs of the educated working professionals?"

It turned out that he was sore that engineers at that time were not getting such starting salaries. His ire was directed especially towards M.A.s and M.Sc.s, whom he regarded as 'inferior' to B.E.s and B.Techs. As for English teachers, he regarded them as the most needless, the most redundant – because anyone could pass an English exam without a teacher's help – or so he imagined!

In her article published in the newspaper, our friend, the English teacher, commented on this attitude of low regard for the teachers. She wrote of her father-in-law, a highly respected Professor of Mathematics, who had retired as Head of the Department of a prestigious college – on the princely, 'last drawn salary' of Rs. 1,500/-.

"If we do not pay our teachers decent, living wages, how can we attract the right people to the teaching profession?" she asked. She also went on to point out that for earnest, sincere teachers, one hour of class often meant two hours of preparation – or even more. They had to spend time in the library, catching up with the latest developments in their subject. They had to devote time to research and further study; they had their share of examination and evaluation work; and, she added, a teacher could not 'switch off' when she left her college and went home for the day. There were always problems to be solved, questions for which answers had to be found; students who had special difficulties and so on. And yet, people felt that teachers should be 'kept in their place'; not paid too much; and worked to the extent possible.

"MPs, MLAs, Managers, Accountants, Judges, Lawyers, Clerks, Policemen and Sweepers are all given the occasional pay-rise and revised scales, and no one raises a murmur," she wrote. "Why is it that our hackles rise when teachers are paid their due?"

People outside the teaching profession are often not aware of the working conditions of teachers and the demands made on them. While this is true of any profession, I cannot help feeling that teachers are particularly vulnerable to such attacks, as their worth and contribution are not often appreciated.

There are several reasons for this. Most teachers are compelled to prepare their students for examinations, rather than provide them with the best possible 'liberal' education. Many teachers are forced to 'lecture' to large, unruly classes for hours together – and if you have not done it, you can have no idea of the tremendous 'expense of the spirit' and sheer physical exhaustion that this involves. When teachers become nervous and harassed, they cannot impart a sense of delight and intellectual pleasure that is to be gained from higher studies, to their students. Thus, frustration and lack of job satisfaction follow.

All right-thinking, right-minded people would agree, that the world needs qualified, dedicated, committed teachers – who are well-treated, well-paid and appreciated, so that they give of their best to the student community and society at large. And I think most of us will agree, that attitudes are changing, and that the teacher is getting his/her due not only in financial terms but also in terms of social esteem.

Let us accept this – a civilised, cultured society must respect its teachers!

Reflect... and Act

Be generous and lavish with appreciation.

Learn to praise:

- All efforts, even if the results are not satisfactory
- All talents and creativity, even though today's education lays emphasis on logic and analytical abilities
- Every positive value exhibited (e.g., sharing, honesty, helpfulness, cheerfulness, etc.)
- All team work, initiative and leadership
- The class as a whole

    (Avoid favouritism. Even if there are exceptionally bright students, it is unfair to single them out for excessive praise.)

In A Lighter Vein

The child comes home from his first day at school. Mother asks, "What did you learn today?"

The kid replies, "Not enough. I have to go back tomorrow."

He who would be a hero, must summon the forces of life to take part in a new drama of action, of service and sacrifice on the battle-field of this earth life.

Sadhu Vaswani

Love : The One Creative Force

A college professor had his class go into the slums to get case histories of 200 young boys. They were asked to write an evaluation of each boy's future. In every case the students studied, he had them follow up on the project to see what had happened to these boys. With the exception of 20 boys who had moved away or died, the students learned that the remaining 180 had achieved more than ordinary success as lawyers, doctors and businessmen.

The professor was astounded and decided to pursue the matter further.

"How do you account for your success?" these men were asked. In each case the reply came with feeling, "There was a teacher."

The teacher was still alive, so he sought her out and asked the old but still alert lady what magic formula she had used to pull these boys out of the slums into successful achievement.

The teacher's eyes sparkled and her lips broke into a gentle smile. "It's really very simple," she said. " I loved those boys."

Believe And Achieve

The society, the public at large, the authorities, the employers may regard you, the teacher, as they choose. What is important is that *you* should hold yourself in high regard. You must not think of yourself as an employee, a paid professional, a hired servant – but as a *guru*, a nation-builder, a character-builder, an instrument of what Swami Vivekananda and Sadhu Vaswani called man-making education.

The Indian heritage, the great ancient tradition of India is yours to claim! This country looked upon its teachers as 'gurus' – people who opened the eyes and minds of their students to a whole world of knowledge.

In the immortal words of Adi Shankara:

> *Ajnana timiraandhasya*
> *Jnaanjana salakaya*
> *Chakshurulmilitam yena*
> *Tasmai Sri Gurave Namah*

I salute the Guru who opens the eyes of one who is blind and veiled by ignorance, applying the collyrium of *jnana* or knowledge.

This tribute is meant for you – and you must take pride in your noble profession. You open the minds of your students to the vast, ever-growing world of knowledge – the realm of light which they can 'see' only with your help and guidance.

You need to cultivate greater self-esteem and self-respect. You need to have greater faith in yourself and in the nobility of your vocation. It would be unfortunate – indeed, disastrous – if our teachers lose their sense of self-worth and self-esteem, and regard their profession as 'lower' than the rest.

What you are doing as a true teacher is character-cultivation; you are helping to create good human beings, good citizens; your contribution is ultimately towards the greater cause of nation-building. When you realise this, surely you will be restored to the sense of nobility and self-worth that you deserve as a teacher.

Our sacred *Upanishads* extol the teaching-learning process as the *tapasya* of knowledge. This great *tapasya* is what you and your students perform, when teaching-learning takes place in the right spirit. This *tapasya* helps your young learners to harness the tremendous powers of inner *shakti* within them, to grow into wholesome, complete, good human beings; it also equips them with the knowledge, wisdom and ability to harness the resources of their natural, cultural and social environment for the benefit of the nation and all humanity.

Therefore, hold your head high! Have faith in yourself ! Swami Vivekananda urged us, again and again, to cultivate the spirit of *atma-shraddha*.

All such ideas as we cannot do *this,* or we cannot do *that,* are superstitions. *Vedanta* teaches men to have faith in themselves first. As certain religions of the world say that a man who does not believe in a personal God outside of himself is an atheist, so *Vedanta* says, a man who does not believe in himself is an atheist. Not believing in the glory of our own soul is what *Vedanta* calls atheism.

Therefore, have faith in yourself, in the nobility of your profession! Believe in yourself! Believe and Achieve!

Reflect... and Act

Share A few Light Moments With Your Class

Once in a while, discard the rigorous formality of the teaching-learning syndrome to spend a few light moments with your students. Let the students do the talking, occasionally. Encourage them to ask questions; to tell you about themselves and their interests, their hopes, their aspirations. Discuss current affairs, explore issues that concern them; play a game or conduct a quiz; listen to what they have to say; they may actually teach you a lot of things you don't know!

A fast growing culture of laughing classrooms has caught up in the western countries. Each day a certain time is set aside for just having fun and laughing. Jokes, tickling tales and funny games are part of the weekly routine. The teachers share with the students the benefits of laughter sessions in the classes:

- o Laughter fills the class with joyful optimism

- o It increases a love for learning

- o It strengthens the bond between the teacher and the students

- o It gives them something to look forward to through the whole day

- o It improves health and immunity

- o It reduces boredom

These sessions will benefit not only them but will help you to see the beauty and charm of life from their youthful, idealistic perspective.

In A Lighter Vein

Little Mohan wasn't getting good marks in school. One day he surprised the teacher with an announcement. He tapped her on the shoulder and said, "I don't want to scare you, but my daddy says if I don't start getting better grades, somebody is going to get a spanking!"

In accepting your duty and living up to it, you will attain true peace and happiness.

Sadhu Vaswani

The Aim Of Education

As an impoverished student and subsequently a struggling lawyer, Abraham Lincoln was often mocked and teased about his habit of constant reading.

"Why do you read so much?" a friend asked him sarcastically. "We can all see that education has not really helped you much in earning a living!"

Lincoln smiled and replied, "I am not educating myself to earn a living...I am trying to find out what to do with a living, if I ever earn it."

Work Not For Wages!

There is an ancient Tao saying: "Choose a job you love – and you won't have to work a day in your life!"

I couldn't agree more! I feel the first secret of success is this – work not for wages, work for the love of work, work for the love of people, work for the love of God! Your work then becomes a source of joy and delight.

I am sure most teachers have chosen to teach because it is a job they love.

There is much talk about vocational education today. The word vocation is derived from the Latin root which means "to call". Let our work be a calling! Let our work be a labour of love, something that we love to do, something that we enjoy doing – rather than just a source of monetary benefit. A labour of love leads to life's greatest fulfillment.

When I visit big cities – perhaps this disease has travelled to smaller cities and towns too – I find that people who are assigned any work always ask, "What's in it for me?" or "What do I get for this?" People work only for wages today. They have forgotten what it is to work with joy, what it is to make their work a source of delight. This is why work has become a cause of so much boredom and so much frustration to many.

Andrew Carnegie, the American industrialist and philanthropist, tells us that there are three types of people in the world: the first type are those who do as little work as possible. The second type are those who do only what their work stipulates – nothing more. But the third type of men, according to Andrew Carnegie, are those who do their duty – and a little more! They are not bound by their office clock. They do not quit at 5p.m. sharp. If there is work to be done, they will stay behind to do it. They do their duty – and a lot more!

In the Bhagavad Gita, which I regard as a Bible of humanity, Lord Krishna expounds His doctrine of *karma yoga*. He tells Arjuna: "Remember – to work you have the right, but not to the fruit thereof." You must work; you must put in your best efforts, you must not slacken your endeavours. But you must not be disappointed, if you do not get the result you seek.

"What is the secret of your success?" they asked a wise man, who had not allowed success to turn his head.

"I pray as if everything depends on God," he said, and added, "I work as if everything depends on me." Don't you think that is a winning formula?

Perhaps many of you will find this unacceptable. You will ask me, "But what about my just compensation? How can anyone work without wages in this world of growing needs?" So let me tell you – of course work and wages go together. They are two sides of the same coin. Whether you work for wages or otherwise, wages are sure to fall into your lap. I am talking about your attitude to work. It is your attitude that will make your life a success or otherwise. And I feel very strongly that your work should be an expression of your love! Those of us who work only for wages will never experience real joy. And when you love your work, you will find it a joy forever.

If we were to face facts, we would soon realise that money is automatically a by-product for those who work well, with sincerity and devotion, and are good at what they are doing. Therefore, dream of the highest, dream of achieving the best that you are capable of. When you work with this attitude, you will never compromise with your values. You will be a teacher, first and last – not just an employee.

May I give you the beautiful words of Khalil Gibran in this connection:

> Work is love made visible.
>
> And if you cannot work with love but only with distaste, it is better that you should leave your work and sit at the gate of the temple and take alms of those who work with joy.
>
> For if you bake bread with indifference, you bake a bitter bread that feeds but half man's hunger.
>
> And if you grudge the crushing of the grapes, your grudge distils a poison in the wine.
>
> And if you sing though as angels, and love not the singing, you muffle man's ears to the voices of the day and the voices of the night.

Work not for wages! Make your work your worship to the Lord. May your God go with you as you work – and you will find that your life and work are both transformed!

Reflect... and Act

It's A Tough Life For A Teacher

Everyone talks about "The Joy of Teaching". But all of us know that it's a tough life!

A teacher shared this story with me sometime ago. She says it has been circulating for years, although nobody can trace its original source.

...Then Jesus took his disciples up to the mountain; and gathering them around him, he taught them, saying:

"Blessed are the poor in spirit, for theirs is the kingdom of heaven.

Blessed are the meek.

Blessed are they that mourn.

Blessed are you when you are persecuted.

Blessed are you when you suffer.

Be glad and rejoice, for great is your reward in heaven."

Was this not teaching at its best? But what if Jesus' students had reacted differently? Consider the following possibility.

And then –

- o Simon Peter said, "Are we supposed to know this?"
- o And Andrew said, "Do we have to write this down?"
- o And James said, "Will we have a test on this?"
- o And Philip said, "I don't have any paper!"
- o And Bartholomew said, "Do we have to turn this in?"
- o And John said, "The other disciples didn't have to learn this!"
- o And Matthew said, "May I go to the bathroom?"

Then one of the Pharisees who was present asked to see Jesus' lesson plan and inquired of Jesus, "Where are your anticipatory set and your objectives in the cognitive domain?"

And Jesus wept.

In A Lighter Vein

Teacher: If I give you two rabbits and two rabbits and another two rabbits, how many rabbits have you got?

Pinky: Seven!

Teacher: No, listen carefully again. If I give you two rabbits and two rabbits and another two rabbits, how many rabbits have you got?

Pinky: Seven!

Teacher: Let's try this another way. If I give you two apples and two apples and another two apples, how many apples have you got?

Pinky: Six.

Teacher: Good. Now if I give you two rabbits and two rabbits and another two rabbits, how many rabbits have you got?

Pinky: Seven!

Teacher: How on earth do you work out that three lots of two rabbits is seven?

Pinky: I've already got one rabbit at home now!

In the coming days, values of character will be regarded as far superior to brain achievements and technological advancements.

Sadhu Vaswani

WHAT OUR STUDENTS MUST BE TAUGHT

Oak – Or Squash?

An impatient father came along with his son – an undergraduate student – to meet James Garfield at Hiram College.

"Look here, Mr. Garfield, my son is very happy to be here in your college. But does his degree programme really have to last three whole years? Can't you shorten the courses so that he might pass out sooner?"

"It all depends on what you want out of his education," Garfield replied. "Even God takes a hundred years to make an oak tree; but a squash takes just two months!"

What Our Students Must Be Taught

Let me give you, once again, the words of Mahatma Gandhi:

> ....we want that education by which character is formed, strength of mind is increased, the intellect expanded, and by which one can stand on one's own feet.
>
> What we need to study, are different branches of knowledge, with it the English language and Western Science, we need technical education, and all else that will develop industries, so that men, instead of seeking service, may earn enough to provide for themselves and save against a rainy day.
>
> The end and aim of all education, all training, should be man-making. The end and aim of all training is to make the man grow. The training by which the power and expression of will are brought under control and become fruitful, is called education.

Beautifully, succinctly, Gandhiji has touched upon the ethical, social and moral values which need to be emphasised in true education!

Alas, the tremendous increase in human knowledge, the enormous advances we have made in science and technology over the last hundred years or so, have unfortunately gone hand in hand with a steep decline in values!

I am sure all of you are aware, that education in India is a costly venture. By current estimates, it costs over one lakh rupees to 'produce' an arts or science graduate; and this 'price' is multiplied several-fold in the case of an engineer, doctor or a technocrat. The fees actually paid by the student represents only a fraction of this cost; the rest is subsidised by the nation – by every tax payer. As we all know, an 'education cess' is now being levied on all tax payers, over and above the revenues already earmarked for education.

This is a tremendous obligation on the students – a moral and social

WHAT OUR STUDENTS MUST BE TAUGHT

responsibility of which most of them are unaware! Each and every undergraduate must be made to realise that his higher education is being obtained at the cost of the tax payer, as part of the tax payers' contribution to national growth and development. If, after obtaining his education, the student fails to repay this debt by serving the society and country through his expertise and training; if he is only interested in making money for himself, then he is no better than a traitor to his nation and his people.

Sadly, many of our young graduates and professionals fall in this category. They constantly complain that the country has done nothing for them; they feel they are unappreciated here; that there is no scope for their talents here, i.e. not enough opportunities to make money.

Recently, I read of a youngster who had passed S.S.C with good grades – and yet attempted suicide, because he could not get his chosen optional subject – IT!

I am reliably informed that many colleges in Pune, now have non-grant sections offering IT to aspiring students – at a price. So, if the parents have deep enough pockets, the youngsters do not have to give in to despair.

Of course, we need to teach our students computer science, biotechnology, business administration, foreign languages, Quantum Physics, software engineering and electronics. But we also need to give them values and ideals without which all these 'subjects' would simply

deteriorate to mere book-learning and fact-cramming!

Thomas Huxley, a collaborator of Charles Darwin, was a distinguished scientist and thinker in his own right. Thomas Huxley pointed out that while Biology teaches us about "the struggle for existence and the survival of the fittest," ethics demands "the fitting of as many as possible to survive."

This contradiction between biological theory and ethical values could not be reconciled easily. The result was that as physical sciences advanced and technological progress was achieved, humanity began to lose sight of its ethical and spiritual values.

Man began to acquire more and more comforts, more and more gadgets, greater power and greater wealth. But human civilisation, as a whole, lost touch with its higher purpose, its direction and motivation. Bertrand Russell expressed this succinctly in his book entitled, *The Impact of Science on Society:*

> ....The machine, as an object of adoration, is the modern form of Satan, and its worship is modern diabolism... Whatever else may be mechanical, values are not, and this is something which no political philosopher must forget....

As I have said to you earlier, modern education has certainly sharpened man's mind; he observed the bird – and he invented the aeroplane; he studied the atom – and he invented the nuclear device; he scrutinised space – and he put together rockets, satellites and spaceships to explore the vast universe.

Man's education and knowledge have indeed taken him far.

As a student of science myself, I am aware that science has bestowed several 'blessings' on mankind. It gave us DDT for killing pests – and we discovered recently that 'pest-free' crops grown with the help of DDT may cause cancer in human beings! And science has given us that fatal equation $e=mc^2$ – and we found that this formula could wipe out entire populations! When men first learnt to split the atom and reveal the tremendous, infinite power that lay within its nucleus, the very first use that they made of this discovery was to rain death and destruction on Hiroshima and Nagasaki. The scientists accused the politicians; the politicians felt they were above accountability; the generals only wanted to win the war – and mankind is yet to live down the shame and tragedy of August 6, 1945, which is truly a black day in human history.

This is the problem with science and technology, when it is not tempered by morality and ethics. Let me repeat, I do not hold science to blame; the problem lies in its misuse.

Maxim Gorkey, the great Russian intellectual, was once addressing a huge rally of peasants. He spoke to them of the rapid strides made by technology; he painted a glorious picture of the various benefits of science. "Look at what science has done for you," he said to them. "Science has taught man how to fly in the air like a bird; science has taught man how to dive into the depths of the ocean like a fish...."

A simple, illiterate peasant in the audience got up and said to him, "Sir, what you say is quite true. Science has taught man how to fly, how to dive into the depths of the ocean and so on. But, unfortunately, there is one thing science has been unable to do – it has not taught man how to live on earth *as a human being*, in peace and goodwill and amity with his fellow-men!"

Is this not the difficulty with scientific knowledge and technological progress? Brain-power has developed considerably; but we need to develop heart-power; we need to give new life to the power of the spirit.

Let me conclude with the words of Bertrand Russell:

> Unless men increase in wisdom as much as in knowledge, increase of knowledge will only be increase of sorrow.

How can we impart wisdom to our students?

Reflect... and Act

Encourage Independent Behaviour:

It is very important to inculcate originality and decision making in our students. One of the repeated complaints against our system is that it stifles creativity and independent thinking, and rewards rote-learning. Also, teachers often complain that their students are passive and not really responsive. But the truth is that students are hardly ever allowed to have their say in the class. They feel they are denied the opportunity to express their views or ideas.

- o Don't expect a "Yes ma'am", "No Sir," response from your students all the time!
- o Let the students make up their own minds on issues that concern them
- o Let them feel free to articulate their views, their choice of the 'right answer"
- o Initiate class discussions on crucial topics
- o Encourage students to raise questions

You must help students to take vital decisions that concern them. This is the way to train them for leadership roles in the future.

In A Lighter Vein

A kindergarten teacher was observing her classroom of children while they were drawing. She would occasionally walk around to see each child's work. As she got to one little girl who was working diligently, she asked what the drawing was. The girl replied, "I'm drawing God."

The teacher paused and said, "But no one knows what God looks like."

Without missing a beat, or looking up from her drawing, the girl replied, "They will in a minute."

The noblest work is to cultivate the soul.

Sadhu Vaswani

Reading And Reflection

A distinguished teacher who met one of his students at the end of the academic year, asked the young man how he was preparing for his examinations.

"I am reading, reading, reading – twelve to fourteen hours, everyday," said the student, earnestly.

"My dear boy," said the Professor, "I strongly advise you to devote six hours to reading and six hours to reflecting on what you have read."

The Evolution Of The Spirit

Let me repeat those powerful words of Bertrand Russell:

> Unless men increase in wisdom as much as in knowledge, increase of knowledge will mean only increase of sorrow....

Is this not the piteous need of today's world – that we need men and women of wisdom, men and women with spiritual strength, *atma shakti!* And who can fashion such a new force, such an enlightened young generation but devoted, committed teachers like you!

Therefore I urge you – do not stop with your 'subject'; do not be content with preparing your students for examinations; do not be satisfied with distinctions and first classes from the university; do not think your job is done when your students are 'placed' in jobs with lucrative salaries; the question you must answer is this: have you prepared them for life? Have you promoted ethical attitudes and moral values? Have you cultivated their character?

This is the best thing about human beings – we are capable of change; we can grow and evolve – intellectually and spiritually. Unlike lesser species, we are not confined to physical change and physical evolution alone: we can grow and evolve on a higher dimension. As teachers, you can be architects of this transformation in your students!

Statistics tell us that India is one of the largest exporters of 'educated manpower' in the world! Our doctors, our nurses, our engineers, our software professionals, our scientists, our professors, our management experts, our mathematicians and economists are respected and valued all over the world. Every year we are turning out more doctors, engineers, lawyers, managers and accountants – let us turn them out as responsible, evolved, ethical, moral beings.

In an international seminar held to mark the centenary of Darwin's Theory of Evolution, Sir Julian Huxley observed:

> In the light of our present knowledge, man's most comprehensive aim is seen not as mere survival, not as numerical increase, not as increased complexity of organisation, or increased control over his environment, *but as greater fulfillment...*

This sense of greater fulfillment is possible only through spiritual growth – and this is what our education must emphasise: for this is the direction that man's evolution must now take.

"True education," Sadhu Vaswani said, "is meant to help us fulfill our destiny, our duty, our mission, our *dharma*. True education is meant to help us fulfill the purpose for which each one of us is here on earth. Therefore, is education a science of life; the art of true living. And the true educator, the true teacher is not just a lecturer or professor: the true teacher is a friend, a guide on the path of life."

Reflect... and Act

Avoid Censure!

Many teachers believe that censure and criticism are essential to discipline the students and to develop a rigorous system of learning. But the truth is, that encouragement, appreciation and a positive outlook are far more effective than censure!

Harsh discipline and criticism may seem to be very effective: a stern warning and a dose of admonition may seem to achieve the desired effect. But criticism and censure only worsen the situation: Criticism –

- o Often tends to be biased
- o Indicates that you don't value your students
- o Shows that your opinion of them is not high
- o Puts off the better students
- o Demoralises the weaker students
- o Leads to self-doubt, in some cases even to low self-esteem
- o Restricts the growth of the class as a whole

Above all, students become wary of a teacher who is always prone to criticising them.

Avoiding censure does not mean abdicating your authority or responsibility as a teacher. Nor does it mean that you put up with indiscipline and shoddy work in class. It only means that you focus on the positive, and treat errors and failures as opportunities for improvement.

In A Lighter Vein

Little Haresh's kindergarten class was on a field trip to their local police station where they saw pictures, tacked to a bulletin board, of the 10 most wanted men.

One of the youngsters pointed to a picture and asked if it really was the photo of a wanted person.

"Yes," said the policeman. "The detectives want him very badly."

So Little Haresh asked, "Why didn't you keep him when you took his picture?"

Youth is hope, not despair. If our beloved and broken India is to be rebuilt, it needs youths full of hope and faith and courage to lay a spiritual foundation of a new nation. Education of the true type has in view, the health and happiness of the whole nation.

Sadhu Vaswani

What We Need To Know

One day, some disciples of Gautama Buddha put to him many questions concerning God. Who exactly was He? How did He manifest? Why did He create human beings? Buddha thought it was a waste of time to consider those questions. His teaching was always direct. He told his disciples a story:

Once upon a time, there lived a man whose house was on fire. As the heat of the flames licked the walls and ceiling, as the black smoke and orange blaze intensified, he continued to sit inside his house. His neighbours, friends and family stood outside, shouting to him, "The wind is blowing! The fire is spreading! What are you doing? Please come out or you will get burnt! You will lose your life."

The man continued to sit where he was and yelled back to them, "What was the cause of the fire? What is the temperature of the fire? What are the chemical constituents of the fire? Unless you give me the answers to these questions, I will not come out."

Buddha told his disciples, "Each of you is like this man. Your house is on fire. The fact is that you are all burning in *trishna,* the fire of desire. You must go and quench the flames. When you have done so, you will reach the state of *nirvana,* enlightenment. Then, all the answers to your questions about God and divinity will become clear to you."

The Art Of True Living

Sadhu Vaswani once asked a gathering of teachers:

> Knowledge is increasing: is happiness increasing, too?
>
> Schools and colleges are multiplying: are happy homes multiplying?

Is not this worth reflecting on?

We have more 'graduates' and 'doctorates' than ever before. Has the nation grown in freshness, vitality and strength? Have our young people become more appreciative of the deeper values which alone can give meaning, and significance to life?

Let us ask ourselves: what constitutes a college or a university?

I am afraid our emphasis is often on *furniture* and *buildings*; or in modern parlance, what is called *infrastructure*.

The college or school or academic institution, as I think of it, is not a *place*, but the *atmosphere* the teachers and students move in. Socrates' School, Plato's Academy and Aristotle's Lyceum were not confined to buildings. Education is, at its best, the fellowship of teachers and students.

And the education we offer in our institutions must equip our students for life – to develop their character, to bring out their individuality, to emphasise their soul-power or *atma shakti*.

Let me give you the powerful message of Swami Vivekananda:

> Each soul is potentially divine; the goal is to manifest this Divine within, by controlling nature, external as well as internal.

This is Swamiji's concept of 'complete' education: we need science and technology, sociology and politics, economics and statistics, mathematics and languages, information technology and business administration, so that we can contribute to social welfare and human progress, but we also need spiritual enrichment and mastery over the self, so that we may move closer to the perfection that each one of us is capable of achieving!

What does this involve?

1. Our students must be taught to love and respect our national heritage, our culture and our ancient Indian values and ideals.
2. Simultaneously, they should be made aware of contemporary life and knowledge – for the modern world too, has a lot to teach us. Our students must be equipped with the capacity whereby they may become worthy contributors to the economic and social wellbeing of the nation.
3. The third and most important dimension would be the application of these two aspects to the cultivation of character – the training of the individual for life.

Our students must be equipped with courage and vision, with culture and courtesy, virtues and graces and values, which alone can make them complete human beings – for it is this alone that can make them mature and emotionally stable men and women, who will learn to live in peace and harmony with their neighbours, with their fellow human beings, with nature and with the mighty forces of this vast universe.

Material advancement – yes; scientific and technological progress – certainly; socio-political efficiency – very essential. But over and above all this, spiritual enrichment, and recognition of the divine potential in each one of us – this alone can be regarded as complete education!

A great thinker and educationist, Gentile, made an illuminating remark: "A school without a spiritual content is an absurdity." And we, in this country, have been trapped in this absurdity for many, many years now!

And let us not wait for our universities, our Boards of Studies and our 'authorities' to introduce a new subject called 'spiritual studies' or a special component called 'character building' into our syllabus!

The spiritual component in education cannot come from without, it already exists in you, the teacher – in the choice you have made to be an educator. Bring this spiritual light to bear upon all that you do – and you will become a true teacher in every sense of that word!

Reflect... and Act

Understanding Behaviour Patterns

Just give it a thought: if you had a class full of the conventional stereotyped 'good' students, all of them quiet, all of them compliant, all of them studious, looking up at you with devotion – wouldn't your life become dull and boring?

Variety is the spice of life! In a single classroom, you may see a kaleidoscope of different personalities. Some may be pleasant, some cannot make their presence felt, some tend to dominate the proceedings – and some are quite unpleasant.

All this categorization takes place because we measure them on our own barometer: we judge them by our perceptions of right and wrong. We insist on our own scale of standardisation.

Our conventional approach may be an impediment in making our students better human beings. Unless we transcend the barriers and the limitations of the mind, we cannot make them bold, courageous, aspiring, energetic and imaginative individuals.

Misbehaviour is every teacher's nightmare! Here are a few ways of working around it:

- o Keep the students busy by assigning challenging tasks, by motivating them to excel -as they say an idle mind is a devil's workshop. The tasks they have at hand should be achievable and they should be able to achieve success in it
- o Keep the mischievous ones in close proximity – they must be aware that you are monitoring them
- o Use rewards – praise as well as tangible rewards for positive behaviour will work wonders
- o Be firm but never angry – there is no place for that emotion in a class room
- o Avoid punishment – it works negatively on the human psyche and is demeaning
- o Maintain a healthy sense of humour – t will lift the tension off the scene, and yet imply that you are a friend in spite of the discipline you are imposing

In A Lighter Vein

When a mother saw a thunderstorm forming in mid-afternoon, she worried about her seven-year-old daughter who would be walking the three blocks from school to home, so she went out to meet her. The lightning was flashing frequently. It wasn't long before the mother saw her little daughter ahead, and she observed that the child was walking nonchalantly along, but whenever lightning flashed, her little girl would stop to smile broadly. Finally, the little girl saw her mother ahead, and the child ran to meet her. "Mother, Mother", she said enthusiastically, "All the way home, God's been taking my picture!"

NOTES

NOTES